BUYING AND RUNNING

a fLORIST SHOP

ALAN PECK

© Alan Peck, 2005
alanpeckpublishing@hotmail.co.uk

Fourth printing 2008

Design and Project Management by Paul Barrett Book Production, Cambridge
Edited by Cambridge Editorial Partnership, Cambridge
Printed by Piggott Black Bear, Cambridge

ISBN 0-9550006-0-2

Contents

Introduction

This is not a book about the artistic aspects of floristry. It is written by someone who has absolutely no design skills and no talent for making anything even remotely attractive from a selection of cut flowers. This is a book about the business side of retail floristry – how to find a suitable business, assess it, purchase it and run it.

It focuses on how to run your business so that you maximise its potential. It is a guide to generating good sales and profitability. It also advises how to build the future value of a business to any prospective purchaser.

My late wife and I owned two different florist shops and we both had very different skill sets. Liz was hugely talented at floristry. I was the businessman who did the books and made many of the deliveries. I also undertook various crucial, unskilled tasks such as washing floors and making tea. Liz was an optimist who charmed customers. She motivated the staff and lit up the shop with her presence and charisma. I am a pessimist who worried about all the financial aspects of the business and getting everything delivered on time.

I am not claiming that we were superstars of the floristry world who made a fortune from it and lived a life of luxury. Like everyone else we made many mistakes – some of our ideas and ventures worked and some did not. Within this book I would like to share the lessons we learned and give guidance on how to tackle all the major aspects of buying and running a florist shop.

Liz first developed an interest in floristry in the 1990s and undertook a course at Hadlow College in Kent. Her enthusiasm grew rapidly as she realised she had a real aptitude for this exciting new interest. When she was presented with the prize as Student of the Year she was hooked.

Rather than Liz seeking employment as a florist working for someone else we bought our first small shop in 1995 in Crayford, Kent. We figured this would enable both of us to learn the different skills we would need if we were eventually to make a living from floristry. With the benefit of hindsight this really was a big gamble. Although it paid off for us I would advise most people to get at least two years' practical experience, ideally working in someone else's shop, before taking the plunge and buying your own business.

Liz ran this shop at a modest profit for four years while we both gained experience and steadily increased the turnover and profitability. At the time I was running an IT business. Doing the shop books and helping with deliveries was a part-time activity for evenings and weekends. Suddenly holidays for all of us, including our children, had to coincide with Christmas, Valentine's Day and Mother's Day as we all became temporary delivery drivers. We sold this business at a good profit in 1999 when we felt we were ready to take on a much larger shop. We needed a business that would generate enough profit to enable me to leave the IT industry. I had tired of commuting after nearly thirty years of long hours and increasing pressure.

Following a lengthy process of checking out many shops for sale in both the UK and the US we eventually bought Biggs Florist in Cambridge. This shop was first established in 1923 and was one of the first members of Interflora. Our main reason for buying it was because it had become stale and tired, yet was still generating good sales and making a modest profit. It was a business we believed had enormous potential. By investing some money in a complete makeover, to give the shop a more modern image, we knew we could make a big improvement.

Fittingly we took over on the first day of the new millennium. Following a chaotic couple of months of building works and administrative hassles we were delighted to find sales rapidly increasing. This only furthered our enthusiasm to try to improve every aspect of the business. Sales continued to climb steadily and the business was providing us with a very comfortable and enjoyable life. We had every intention of keeping it until we were well into our dotage, but in 2004 disaster struck.

In January 2004 we took our usual post-Christmas holiday. Liz had been feeling unwell and our aim was to recover from Christmas and unwind before the build up to Valentine's Day. We spent two weeks in a waterfront villa next to a golf course in Antigua. We settled into a routine of playing golf every morning followed by a couple of beers and a bite to eat in the clubhouse. This was followed by an afternoon of swimming and sunbathing by the pool before going out to a good restaurant for the evening. Life seemed great and I tried to convince myself that she had shaken off whatever had been troubling her.

Liz seemed to lack her usual drive and enthusiasm for the Valentine's Day and Mother's Day peak periods. We then took another short golfing holiday in March. As Liz was still able to play eighteen holes of golf I thought there could not be anything too serious wrong with her.

For some time Liz had been visiting her GP and having numerous blood tests. It was thought she had probably picked up a persistent bug and that she should take things easier at the shop. However, in April Liz suffered a stroke. She was admitted to the Medical Assessment Unit in Addenbrookes Hospital in Cambridge for tests.

Following a month of tests and incorrect diagnoses the doctors delivered chilling news to both of us. Liz had cancer – the primary cancer was in the pancreas and secondary cancer had spread to the liver. Late that night I drove home in shock and despair. I sat up all night surfing the net to see what I could learn about pancreatic cancer. To my horror I found that the survival rate was less than one per cent. It was almost certain that there was no hope of survival.

Liz was allowed to come home to our little farm cottage. It was obvious that there was very little more that could be done, other than making her last days as comfortable as possible. I spent most of my time caring for her with the help of nursing assistance from the wonderful Hospice At Home service provided in Cambridge. We decided that we would put the business on the market, hoping that a quick sale would enable me to care for Liz full time. I also knew that working in the shop could never be the same again for me without Liz. I would eventually need to do something completely different.

Fortunately there were lots of prospective buyers. In what seemed like no time at all we had accepted an offer for the full asking price and the deal was done. The sale of the shop was completed on Friday, 20th August 2004. Just three days later Liz stopped breathing while the nurse and I were at her bedside. I was puzzled that the nurse was pointing out of the window. Then I saw that on an overcast day there was a sudden break in the cloud that allowed the sun to light up the cornfield outside. I knew the end had come.

Liz had planned her funeral to the last detail and was buried under her favourite copper beech tree in the tiny village cemetery. She had given Jo, the shop manager, detailed instructions for the make-up of a lily spray to go on top of her coffin. The girls in the shop had to work until 10pm on the night before the funeral to make up the many orders that came in from family, friends and other florists. The church was packed and on a sunny August day we all said our goodbyes.

At the time of writing this, several months have passed. In this time I cried buckets and wrote over a hundred letters to well-wishers. I finalised all the administration relating to the sale of the shop and wondered what on earth I was going to do without the woman I loved so much.

I decided to write this book as a tribute to Liz. It is also an attempt to give something back to an industry that gave us the best ten years of our life. I see people entering the business with very little idea of how to buy and run a florist shop in a way that will provide an appropriate return for their initial investment. I hope this book will help those people to avoid many common mistakes and to maximise the potential of their shop.

I need to thank a number of people, particularly my daughter Helen, my son Chris, his fiancée Jana and Liz's sister Scilla. They all helped to nurse Liz through the darkest of days and supported me as I struggled to cope with being both a carer and shop owner. I love them all dearly.

I also need to thank 'the girls' who pretty much ran the shop on their own for the last four months of Liz's life. So to Jo, Vicky, Hazel, Michelle, Alison, Dawn, Bonnie and Sarah, thank you for being a fantastic team of florists. You always did whatever was needed, worked long hours, met the deadlines, put up with my demands and took the mickey out of me when I deserved it. Despite the pressures, we always had a good laugh and Liz and I always thought of you as very good friends rather than as members of staff. I love you all.

Finally I must stress that, despite all the help I have had with proofreading and with compiling this book, any errors are entirely my fault and my responsibility.

1 Finding the right shop

This chapter looks at:

Starting your own florist business

At the time of our first purchase Liz had been studying floristry for a year and preparing for her Intermediate Certificate of the Society of Floristry (ICSF) exams. Her tutor had expressed amazement at the speed with which Liz was learning the essential skills of floristry. I had never seen her so enthusiastic about anything before. Every evening she continued studying at home, asking me to test her on both the common and the Latin names of flowers and plants.

I was working for a large American computer business. My base office was in Old Windsor. Commuting was a 110-mile round trip on the M25 from our home in Kent and I had been making the journey for some years. With frequent business trips to the US and Europe, I was beginning to tire of this existence. The pressures of satisfying the Board of Directors that I was meeting all my financial targets were slowly grinding me down.

My job involved full budgetary responsibility for running the company's Education Centres around Europe at a profit. I was involved in many meetings with accountants and much of my time was spent examining financial spreadsheets. Almost without realising it, I was acquiring all sorts of general business skills that would prove to be useful in running a small business. I was also examining business plans put to me by my staff. I had to assess whether they had properly identified all the costs and, crucially, to decide whether their sales projections were realistic and achievable. I was later to find this experience invaluable when I started to study the profit and loss statements of florist shops.

Liz had been planning to acquire the basic skills of floristry at college before then seeking a job as a florist. However, as her enthusiasm grew she floated the idea of buying her own shop. Liz had some previous retail experience and believed she could handle the floristry if I could handle the administrative work and do the books.

The more I thought about it the more it appealed. We could afford to buy a small business and use it as the first step to a new future. It might eventually enable me to leave the IT industry. I could work with Liz in a completely different industry. We assumed that profits would be minimal in our first shop but that we would spend a few years learning the essential skills needed in the floristry world, while my main job effectively subsidised us. We were confident that we would at least recoup our initial investment when we were ready to sell the business and would be able to afford to move on to something bigger.

We began the search for our first business by contacting various business transfer agents. We studied the small ads in our local newspapers, *Florist & Wholesale Buyer* magazine and *Daltons Weekly*. We also looked at what little relevant material existed on the Internet at that time.

I quickly realised that we were each focusing on quite different aspects of the businesses for sale in our area. Liz was primarily looking at the appearance and location of shops. She was imagining what she could do to improve them. I was looking much more at the financial aspects. I wondered how some of these small shops could even cover their costs with such tiny volumes of sales.

We found a small shop in a parade next to Crayford rail station in Kent. It was just five miles from our home and seemed to fit the bill. Turnover was modest but it was a clean and tidy little shop that was being run by the owner with part-time help. Examination of the accounts showed a small, but realistic, net profit. After some negotiation our offer was accepted and Liz became the very excited and proud owner of Blooms of Crayford.

When I looked back at this first purchase in later years I frequently searched for lessons we had learned from it. My main memory is of the day we completed the sale and the business was handed over to us. It was a Friday and Liz had spent the day in the shop with the previous owner, doing a stock check and finding out where everything was and how things worked. I arrived at the shop at 5pm and asked all the questions I could think of. I concentrated on the admin aspects of the shop, in particular how the Teleflorist relay orders were processed. At 6.30pm we shook hands with the previous owner and her husband and they left, never (we assumed) to be seen again, although we were mistaken because, after some months, she returned as an occasional customer.

I clearly remember Liz and I standing in the shop and looking at each other on that Friday evening, realising that at 8.30 the following morning we had to be open for business and that, apart from a Saturday girl, we were on our own.

Amazingly, and to be honest, luckily things went well. Our Saturday girl Monica proved to be a very savvy, likeable girl. She was also a competent, if inexperienced, florist. Liz also took on Miriam and Val, friends and fellow students at Hadlow College, as part-time florists.

I made all the deliveries on that first Saturday in our little Suzuki van. I then spent the Sunday on admin and setting up a basic accounting system. I had booked a week's holiday from work. This enabled me to spend a full first week getting to grips with the many facets of a small business operating in an industry that was completely new to me. I returned to work a week later in very high spirits. I was convinced that I could see a way out of the IT world to a more enjoyable future.

Starting your own florist business? Checklist

Before you consider starting your own florist business there are some points to consider that are basic to starting any business:
- ✓ What skills do you have?
- ✓ Could you adapt your existing skills?
- ✓ Could you turn your passion into a business?
- ✓ What type of person are you?
- ✓ What are your personal circumstances?
- ✓ Can you afford to do it?
- ✓ Are you suited to self-employment?
- ✓ Do you have the patience and application necessary to research your idea thoroughly?

Working with a partner

It quickly became apparent that Liz's and my completely different skill sets were actually a very good combination for such a small business. Had we both been florists with no general business skills or business people without floristry skills, it would have been a disaster. It also helped that Liz was much more of an extrovert and an eternal optimist. I was far more cautious and always worried that, unless we were very careful and worked very hard, sales would fall, costs might get out of control and we would fail to deliver the right products to the right places on the right days.

I think every business benefits from a combination of personalities. If everyone is an optimist, potential problems are not identified until they become real problems. If everyone is a worrier then the flair and imagination needed continually to generate new ideas and products is likely to be lacking.

Unlike Liz, I am a morning person. I like to get up early and I have lots of energy and enthusiasm for a long morning's work. Liz hated getting up in the morning and would be very quiet for the first hour or two of the day. Then she would steadily gain in energy and enthusiasm as the day went on. Often I would feel exhausted at the end of the day while Liz would decide it was time to start washing the shop floor.

We had been worried about how we would get on as husband and wife working together on a permanent basis. As things turned out this was not a problem. In fact our skills and our roles in the shop were so different that they kept us apart for most of the day. While Liz was serving customers, or doing make-up work, I would be out delivering or in our little office doing admin work. At the end of the day we loved to talk about what had happened during the day and what was planned for the following day.

We were partners in the husband and wife sense but any two people with complementary skills could make a venture work. There are many talented florists without business skills who have acquired their own shop and prospered because they have had the good sense to find someone else with the right business skills to work very closely with them. Conversely there are business people without floristry skills who have been equally successful. They have taken on talented and experienced florists who have also proved to be totally honest and trustworthy.

Working with a partner? Checklist

✓ Are you compatible?
✓ Do you have matching/complementary skills?
✓ Do you have an equal commitment to the business?
✓ Do you agree on your aims for the business?
✓ Can you work as a team?

The right location

The location of a shop is one of the most critical factors in assessing the viability and the value of any given business. A town centre location with high pedestrian flow (footfall) is always likely to generate a high volume of walk-in sales. The downside is that the rent will almost certainly reflect this. A location on the edge of town may have a much lower rent but also a much smaller level of walk-in sales.

If a shop is not in a town centre then it can make a difference which side of the road it is on. It is generally considered that a florist shop will do better if it is on the 'going home' side of the road. This is because people are more likely to buy flowers on the way home, rather than on the way to work.

A location right on a corner can be a problem as the busyness of the road junction can require all of a driver's concentration. If a driver is very busy looking at side roads and other vehicles there is no time for taking in anything else. However, if the road is so busy that the traffic is often stop-start this can be an advantage, particularly if you have your own parking. When people are stuck in traffic they are much more likely to look at the shops on either side. Some shops situated on a busy but free-running road often go unnoticed, even by regular commuters.

> Our second shop, in Cambridge, was on the outskirts of town but still had plenty of walk-in customers. This was because it had good parking on its own forecourt and overflow parking at the rear of the shop. Many customers would shop in Cambridge city centre but call in at the shop on their way home to buy flowers. People did not want the inconvenience of walking around the town centre with a bouquet of flowers.

As the years passed we found that a larger and larger percentage of our business was coming in via the telephone, the Internet and through the Interflora computer system. Thus we became less and less reliant on walk-in sales and pleased that we were not tied in to a long and expensive city centre lease. However, this is not to say that everyone should avoid town centres. If the volume is great enough and the rent reasonable enough then it can work very well.

Although it is very desirable to have parking for both customers and staff this is usually impossible in a busy central location and delivery by wholesalers using huge lorries can be a nightmare. I always enjoyed being on the edge of town with lots of parking and easy access. However, I have always known there was a price to pay for this.

The right location? Checklist

When considering any location, make sure you check:
✓ Accessibility for customers and suppliers.
✓ Parking.
✓ Pedestrian flow past premises.

Leasehold or freehold?

Most existing businesses will be for sale on a leasehold basis rather than freehold. Freehold will clearly be more expensive but if you are prepared to undertake a big enough change in circumstances this can be attractive.

You may have the option of either taking over the balance of an existing lease or taking out a new lease. It used to be the case that stamp duty on a new lease was a minimal amount. At the time of writing it has become 1 per cent of the rent due over the full term of the lease, although for small businesses there is a threshold before this kicks in. For a really large shop and a long lease this can amount to a sizeable sum.

Taking over the balance of an existing lease will make the purchase quicker and easier and should eliminate your liability for stamp duty. The problem is it also reduces your security of tenure. This may seem only a small gamble if the freeholder can convince you that all they want is a reliable tenant who will pay their rent on time and undertake repairs according to the terms of the lease. Many freeholders are only too pleased to continue the *status quo* with a reliable tenant. They enjoy not just the rental income but also the knowledge that the property is steadily gaining in value.

> With our second shop, we took on responsibility for an elderly, tired-looking property so we decided to spend some money on a surveyor. He produced a 'Schedule of Condition' for the premises at the time that we were negotiating the lease. This involved producing a detailed report on the condition of the property, including photographs of all the weak points such as signs of damp, damaged flooring or suspect woodwork.
>
> This cost us some £600 but it gave us great peace of mind. We knew that we could use it to fight any unjust claims for damages when we eventually vacated the premises.

A long lease gives you the security of knowing that you will not have to find new premises for a long time. If the owner of the freehold should ultimately decide to use the premises for a different purpose this will be a problem. I would advise any prospective leaseholder to find as much information as they can about the freeholder.

We did not do this sufficiently well when we bought our first shop. We then experienced lots of problems with a rogue landlord whom the police were frequently making enquiries about. With the freeholder of our second shop we had a very friendly relationship, and never a cross word, with a very honourable and trustworthy landlord.

The state of repair of the property should always be assessed to enable you to estimate the cost of repairs and improvements. Also think about the running costs of heating and lighting the premises.

Leasehold or freehold? Checklist

Investigate:
✓ The landlord.
✓ The advantages and disadvantages of a new lease.
✓ Running costs.
✓ Likely repair costs.
✓ A 'Schedule of Condition'.

Making the choice

When we were searching for our second shop we had just sold our house in Kent and I was preparing to leave the IT industry for good. We helped our children to move out and buy their own property. We were in a situation where we could move anywhere where we could find a suitable shop to purchase.

Our first choice was to move to the United States, either to Florida or the Carolinas. Having worked for an American company for most of my life I had made many trips to the States and Liz had accompanied me several times.

Over a period of a couple of years we had been researching floristry in the US and had long subscribed to the American equivalent of the *Florist Magazine*. Every time we went over there we called at all the local florist shops. We chatted to staff and owners who were always more than happy to give advice.

Once we were ready to make the move we drew up a list of ten businesses for sale in Florida. This was eventually narrowed down to a short list of four that were big enough concerns to enable us to qualify for an E2 Treaty Investor visa. We visited each of these businesses, meeting the owners and studying the books. We found that there were problems with the finances of at least three of them and our shortlist was reduced to one.

Our one remaining hope was a pleasant-looking shop in Ocala that seemed to be in healthy financial shape. But there was a problem: the agents and owners could not provide all the details I was asking for. Only when I told them that there was no way we would make an offer without all the accounting details did they finally come up with the missing information. As soon as I saw it I knew why they had withheld it (see chapter 2, *Checking the books*).

At this point we decided to give up the idea of moving to the US. Every business we looked at either had some fundamental problem, or a financial skeleton in the cupboard, that made the purchase too big a risk. We decided to concentrate our search on the UK.

Our next decision was whether to buy an existing business or to start a new business from scratch.

Starting from scratch

Starting from scratch can seem very appealing. All the money you would otherwise pay for an existing business can be channelled into the start up of a new venture. You could create your own shop with an image and name of your choice.

If you divide the population of the UK by the number of florist shops, the average population per shop works out to approximately 7,000. If you could find a small town with such a population, suitable vacant shop premises and no florist shop then this is a possibility. However, a great deal will depend on the town. An affluent local population in a prosperous area is obviously a much better bet than a rundown area. There are towns with populations half the quoted average with a thriving local florist. Conversely there are towns with twice the average population and perhaps just one florist sandwiched between empty boarded up shops.

Another factor is local competition. Greengrocers, corner shops, garages and out-of-town supermarkets, will all sell inexpensive cut flowers. Then there are the many other people who sell cut flowers from private houses, market stalls and vans at the side of the road. Most florist shops now sell very few bunches of cut flowers. They make their money from producing customised bouquets and arrangements for the many special occasions when a cheap bunch from a supermarket will not suffice.

We found that many of our customers readily admitted that they had got into the habit of buying an inexpensive bunch of flowers as part of their regularly weekly bulk shopping from an out-of-town supermarket. They saw us as the people to contact when they wanted something special for a birthday, anniversary or funeral or to thank someone for something. We decided that rather than get mad at supermarkets muscling in on the floristry sector we would take a wider view. We figured that they were helping to make flower buying a regular consumer purchase and we could benefit from the spin-off from this.

Start-ups are usually less risky in a larger town where there are already a number of existing florist shops. However you must convince yourself there is room for one more. To do this you have to be sure that you can either fill a niche in the market or that you can take a lot of trade from existing shops. This can be very tough if the competition is doing a good job. If some shops are shabby and tired, and the current owners have lost enthusiasm, this can provide opportunities.

Whether starting from scratch, or buying an existing shop, you should always think about the risks relating to the size of the town and the population. If you have the only florist shop in a small town you could be at enormous risk if a competitor opens up across the street. However if you own one of ten florist shops in a large town the risk is obviously much less if an eleventh shop opens up.

If you can find a location where you have a realistic chance of building a viable business this can be a very exciting venture. It is an opportunity to design and furnish a shop exactly as you want it with new signage, marketing literature, a website and so on. The problem is, of course, the time it takes to establish and build a new business from scratch. Even a lovely new shop that is well marketed and stocked with a wide variety of beautiful flowers and plants will struggle in the early days. Before we bought our first shop I can remember a wise old florist advising me to write down all of the many things I thought we would need to spend money on. Then to add it all up, take the total, and double it. This turned out to be very good advice.

Typically a new business will lose a lot of money in the first year. It will continue to make significant losses in the second year. If the owners have done a great job and chosen the location wisely they might get close to break-even in the third year. There will be a few who buck this trend but many more that do not. It is a statistical fact that most new small businesses of this type close down within the first three years.

Whether you decide to start from scratch or buy an existing business, you will need access to significant funds. With an existing business most of your funds will go towards purchase costs. With a start-up venture a similar amount of money will probably be required to cover the losses you will make in the first three years. You have to make the choice very carefully.

Starting from scratch? Checklist

If you are considering a start up business, consider the following points.

✓ Will you be leaseholder or freeholder?
✓ Is the location suitable?
✓ Is the building suitable?
✓ Will you need planning permission for any alterations?
✓ Are the premises in a high crime area?

✓ Talk to other local shopkeepers about the area.
✓ Research the competition in the area.
✓ Visit the area at different times of the day on different days of the week.
✓ What development plans are there in the area?

Buying an existing business

When we decided to look for our second shop, we put a lot of work into finding a good location for a start-up but just could not find one we felt confident about. We then concentrated all our efforts on finding an established business. We were looking for a relatively large shop, in terms of turnover, and one that was making a reasonable profit. We were also looking for something with lots of potential. We wanted to improve and develop a business with a realistic level of investment.

I was still working full-time so we visited a different area every weekend to check out any florist shops for sale. We did research through agents during the week and arranged viewing appointments for the weekend. After a while, however, we began to think we were searching for the impossible. We looked at so many shops with shaky accounts. This always ruled them out in my view, even if Liz thought the shop had potential. Conversely we looked at some shops that had good accounts and were being superbly run by dynamic owners. Often this enabled them to command a high price that we felt was too much for us.

If the business is already being superbly run, you have to consider honestly whether you can maintain the standards set by the current owners. Most of the tired-looking shops had terrible accounts and most of the impressive shops with good books were too expensive.

Some owners decide not to let the staff know when they are putting a business up for sale and are careful not to have the shop advertised in an identifiable way. They arrange viewings outside shop hours when no staff are around. This is understandable if the owners do not want to unsettle the staff, or if they fear that staff would feel under threat and start looking for alternative employment. In my experience staff are usually very wary of new owners and seem to take the view of 'better the devil you know'.

We finally found what we were looking for in Cambridge. Biggs & Sons was the longest-established florist in Cambridge and occupied large but tired-looking premises on the very busy main road leading from Cambridge out towards Ely. The shop frontage had very old signage and a rickety old lean-to projecting from above the shop windows. This greatly reduced the natural light in the shop itself. However, it was well situated approximately half way between the city centre and the Cambridge Science Park.

Turnover was at a good level but had hardly grown at all for the past three years. This still enabled the business to make a modest but genuine net profit. It had been in the Biggs family since 1923. A combination of advancing years, and the lack of another son or daughter who really wanted to manage the shop, had convinced the owner the time had come to hand over to someone else.

The Biggs family had done a great job in building up a large and loyal customer base. They had been one of the very first members of Interflora and there was still memorabilia in the shop relating to the very early days of the organisation.

Before making an offer we revisited the shop at different times of the day. We parked covertly on the opposite side of the road to observe walk-in trade. We were amazed at the number of people who walked into this very uninviting looking shop and walked out having bought something. This was what finally convinced us to buy.

It was so easy to see how, with a relatively modest investment, we could give this shop a completely fresh new image. We realised we had to do this without alienating the many long-established customers. They kept returning to the shop despite its faded appearance and were clearly happy with both the service and the quality they were receiving.

There are huge advantages to buying an existing business. When a business is already up and running, you can concentrate on building up profits and business development. The systems will already be in place (suppliers, staff and equipment) and there will be an established client base. If relations are good (and there is no reason why they should not be) you can benefit from the advice and experience of the previous owners – and the financial history of an existing business can be fully examined on request.

Buying an existing business? Checklist

Before you make an offer on an existing business:

✓ Examine the financial health of the business.

✓ Will you need planning permission for any alterations?
✓ Consider commissioning a surveyor's report.
✓ Are the premises in a high crime area?
✓ Talk to other local shopkeepers about the area.
✓ Research the competition in the area.
✓ Observe the premises at different times of the day on different days of the week.
✓ What development plans are there in the area?

Assessing the vendor

As well as checking out the shop it is also essential to try to assess the current owners and their reasons for selling. It is important to feel that you really trust the vendors and that what they tell you is verified when you check out the details in the books.

It is also important to find out what other business interests the vendors have. If they are clearly enjoying a good standard of life is this because of the success of the shop or do they have other means of income? It is quite possible for someone owning more than one shop to channel sales from other shops into a poorly performing shop that they would like to dispose of. If they also put some of the stock purchases through their other shops then it is easy to show a healthy profit in the books of their weakest shop. This makes it possible to sell a poorly performing shop for a very good price. The likelihood is that this shop may not even survive as a competitor to their other shops, especially if the previous owner then targets their old customer base.

Many small shops are effectively subsidised by the owner's partner having alternative employment. Although Liz made a consistent profit from her first small shop there was no way it could have provided both of us with a living. This is the case with many businesses in this industry. At conferences we met many couples like us where one partner was a florist and the other had a completely different background. The partner would usually contribute to the business by handling the admin and helping with deliveries.

For a couple to have any real hope of making a living from a florist shop it has to have reached a certain critical mass in terms of the level of sales turnover. I came to the conclusion that no couple can enjoy a good standard of living with an annual turnover of less than at least £250,000 – unless they have some means of acquiring stock at very low cost and/or have unusually low overheads.

Many shops are advertised for sale where one glance at the essential details of stated turnover, rent, gross profit, etc. reveals that the owner cannot be making more than a tiny net profit. However, shops like this still sell. There are clearly many who dream of owning their own florist business. This can often make a florist shop much easier to sell than other businesses where potential buyers are focused on taking a hard-headed look at the finances.

Assessing the vendor? Checklist

✓ Find out as much about the vendor as possible.

✓ Is the vendor trustworthy?

✓ Are the reasons for the sale of the business convincing and genuine?

✓ What other business interests does the vendor have?

✓ Make sure you have full access to the business accounts.

✓ Take independent advice about the business accounts if necessary.

✓ Have a realistic idea of the annual turnover you need.

Adjusting to self-employment

Over the years many customers told us that they thought it must be lovely to own a shop like ours and have the opportunity to work with flowers all day. I often wondered if they would feel the same if they were buying stock inside a refrigerated Dutch lorry at 6am on a Saturday in January or washing the shop floor on a Sunday morning. But we understood their enthusiasm. We wanted to spend lots of time in the shop.

Having spent most of our lives as salaried employees we found the whole concept of self-employment and being employers ourselves difficult to get used to.

When we took over Biggs Florist the staff were extremely unsure about us. Once we took over and started to make improvements this quickly changed. We found they were struggling to work with blunt scissors and knives. They sat on stools in the workroom that were so old the metal frames were protruding through the cushioned seats. Things like this we fixed in the first week. Then when we started to modernise the whole shop, and improve the wages, this lifted everyone's morale and the girls welcomed us with open arms. When, a few years later, we finally sold the Cambridge shop we decided to tell all the staff before we put it on the market. We felt this was only fair and that it would be easier to cope with any concerns they might have sooner rather than later. Also we knew that we had an attractive shop to sell. This was well known to the many people who were likely to be interested. We wanted everyone to be able to identify the shop easily when it was advertised.

If you do take over a shop and make the mistake of alienating the staff you can quickly find yourself in a nightmarish situation with costs rising, orders going wrong, unhappy customers and your investment rapidly diminishing in value. Florists do not take kindly to a new owner criticising their make-up work, especially if they know that person cannot do as good a job themselves.

If the shop has a proven track record of rising sales and good profits then this can only be because the staff have been doing a great job. All businesses are a direct reflection of the capabilities of the staff employed. It is possible for a failing business to employ good staff but not the reverse. If the business has consistently performed well then the staff must be good. Why endanger your investment by taking a heavy-handed approach and letting people know that they had better toe the line?

Day-to-day delegating can also be difficult for the newly self-employed. When we first took over Biggs, we had days when Liz and I were rushed off our feet in the shop but leaving some of the girls without enough work to do. This understandably frustrated them. On the other hand, we felt it was unfair if the staff were putting in more hours than we were and that there was a need for us not to be thought to be slacking. This is ridiculous because if there are enough staff for the given workload, and the shop is running efficiently, you should feel quite comfortable about taking as much time off as you want. On some relatively quiet days, when we had plenty of staff in the shop, the girls would implore Liz and me to take the day off. There were times when they literally pushed me out of the shop and insisted that I go to the golf course.

I have to admit that I have not always followed my own good advice. In our early days at Biggs Florist I could get very stressed while making deliveries on a busy day and the girls used to joke about needing to 'get their tin hats out'. One day, after I had stormed out of the shop in a temper with a batch of orders, I eventually returned to the shop to find all the girls were really wearing tin hats (upturned bowls used for arrangements). This was a great idea on their part as we all had a good laugh and I felt completely stupid and learned a valuable lesson.

The girls often did things like this and on reflection I am grateful that they were so patient with me when I was being so difficult to work with. Whenever I was the butt of their jokes it was because I deserved it. I like to think that at least I usually had the good grace to say I was sorry and buy them all cream cakes. Mind you, the cakes often got me into yet more trouble because of the girls' diets...

Many shops for sale include living accommodation, usually a flat above the shop. When I was spending hours commuting around the M25 every day, the idea of living above my job often seemed like heaven but there is a downside to consider. It may eliminate commuting and be good for security, but do you really want to be permanently accessible to your staff? No matter how much you tell your staff that you are taking a day off and are not available, they will be calling up the stairs whenever there is a problem.

When Liz took a day off she loved to spend a day in town, shopping and lunching, with her mobile switched off. I liked to spend a morning on the golf course or an afternoon at a football match – again with the mobile turned off. I know many owners who would never dream of switching their mobile off in case of some emergency at the shop. But we always believed in having some strictly private leisure time to ourselves – and we knew we could rely on our staff to look after the shop while we were away.

Adjusting to self-employment? Checklist

Becoming self-employed and an employer after being an employee for years can present unforeseen problems.

✓ You are the boss.
✓ Pace yourself.
✓ Do not forget that there is life outside the shop.
✓ Make and maintain an open relationship with your staff.
✓ Do not forget to delegate.
✓ Remember that you are allowed time off.

2 Checking the books

This chapter looks at:

- Confidentiality agreements
- Examining the accounts
- Financing your purchase
- Sole traders, partnerships and limited companies
- Using an accountant
- Level of sales and profits

- Checking the costs
- Inspecting the paperwork
- Gross profits and mark-ups
- Claims of unrecorded sales
- Assessing the value of a business
- Making an offer

Having found a business that appears to fit your needs the next step is to obtain as much information as you can about the accounts. The first step is to ask for the last three years' accounts. This must include a full set of profit and loss statements.

Confidentiality agreements

If there is a business transfer agent working on behalf of the seller they will want you to view the shop first and meet the owners. If they are satisfied that you are a serious prospective purchaser they will usually require you to sign a non-disclosure agreement before they will allow access to any accounting details. This is partly to avoid timewasters but also to guard against the vendor's competitors gaining valuable information. If you are a serious prospect but still have difficulty getting access to accounting information, you should immediately be suspicious.

Examining the accounts

Before a large company finalises the purchase of another company it will first carry out the due diligence process. They often involves a small army of accountants verifying the true financial position of the company to be purchased. They will examine all of the costs and the current and future liabilities. They check the security of forward orders and the base of account customers. Every aspect has to be checked to guard against the risk of paying too much for a business.

You will not need a small army of accountants if you are thinking of buying a business but you certainly will need the help of an accountant. You should also seek advice and guidance from someone with real experience of owning a florist shop.

In chapter 1 I wrote about a shop we were interested in buying in Ocala, Florida. The shop looked right, the owner seemed like a nice guy and we met all the staff. They seemed to be happy, efficient and well motivated. The big problem was the accounts. Getting the information that I wanted from the broker representing the owner was like pulling teeth.

He eventually provided profit and loss statements, verified by the owner's accountant, covering a period of two years and ending some fifteen months previously. These looked okay at first glance but what I really wanted were details of the last full financial year and this became a real problem. We were negotiating just after the end of that year and the broker claimed, not unreasonably, that he could provide quarterly details but that the full year-end accounts were not yet complete.

Liz and I returned to the broker's offices the following day where he presented us with quarterly details for the first, second and fourth quarters. Bizarrely, the accounts for the third quarter were missing.

When we asked for the missing quarter he said the owner couldn't find them but that we shouldn't worry, as the missing quarter was very similar to the other quarters. I explained that this was totally unacceptable. We couldn't possibly make an offer without access to the whole of the last year's accounts. Liz and I returned to our hotel having told the broker either to produce the missing details or to expect never to see us again. That evening the broker called us to say that the missing information had been found and would be available for us at his office the following morning. I did the all the provisional sums, ready to add the missing quarter.

Assuming that the missing information was in line with what we had been told, and that we could verify this, Liz and I agreed on an offer we would make for the business. We had also been looking at houses in the area: the funds were all in place and provisional visa arrangements made. Liz and I set off for the broker's offices the following morning fully expecting to make a formal offer and lodge a deposit. We were both full of enthusiasm at the prospects of an exciting new life in the United States.

As soon as I saw the missing third quarter's accounts I knew immediately why they had been so difficult to get hold of. Sales had been very disappointing in that quarter. All sorts of stock costs, and exceptional annual costs, had been shoehorned into that one quarter in an attempt to make the other three quarters look really good. I added the missing quarter to the other three, to come up with a provisional profit and loss for the year as a whole. The picture of the business was now completely different, with a net profit that simply wasn't good enough.

When I explained this to the brokers and said we most certainly would not be making an offer they looked at their feet and were clearly embarrassed. Amazingly, before we left their offices they asked if I would be interested in working for them as a broker instead. I suppose this was some sort of compliment!

This was a clumsy and obvious attempt to deceive us. However, I have seen people from the UK make quite incredible purchases of businesses in both Florida and the UK. Unfortunately there are a lot of prospective purchasers around who are so carried away by their dreams that they are prepared to believe everything they are told.

Examining the accounts? Checklist

✓ Employ an accountant.
✓ Take advice from an experienced retailer.
✓ Demand full access to the company accounts, including
  • profit and loss for the previous 3 years
  • profit and loss for the last full financial year
  • tax liabilities for the company.
✓ Investigate any outstanding loans made to the business.
✓ Consider employing an agent to do an independent evaluation of the business.

Financing your purchase

Before you start to look for a business you will obviously have to have some idea of how you will finance any purchase. In addition to the purchase price, there are legal fees and all sorts of start-up costs to calculate. You will also need sufficient reserves to avoid any cash flow problems.

Within the first few days of taking over a floristry business you will receive invoices for all sorts of essential services, including shop insurance, buildings insurance, vehicle insurance, telephone line rental, credit card processing services and possibly joining fees for a relay service. There will also be the first demands for rent, rates and water, etc. The relay service will usually retain some of the monies due to you in the first six months by way of a deposit. They will retain this money for however long you are a member.

Your wholesale suppliers may insist on immediate payment to start with. When they get to know you better and confidence is established they will usually allow you to pay on account. Account customers whom you invoice will not pay straight away. Some will take up to three months or even more. You have to start with enough funding to see you through these difficult early days. It will seem that lots of money is going out and far less is coming in.

Few people have enough surplus personal cash to go out and buy a business outright. However, thanks to the property booms of the 1980s and the 1990s, many people have enough equity in their houses to enable them to fund all sorts of projects. If you are not in this position and have to borrow the money required, then the bank, or whoever is providing the finance, will almost certainly need very good security. Typically this means your house has to be used as collateral, before they will advance the money.

> We bought our first shop for cash but it was only small and we were able to fund it from our personal savings. Had we wanted to remain in our house, we would have had to borrow money to buy a larger shop. So we concentrated on paying off the mortgage as early as we possibly could and building equity for the future.
>
> Following several years of hard saving we finally reached a situation where we had paid off the mortgage and sold both the house and the first shop. We now had enough money to buy a house and business in Cambridge and still be able to keep a sizeable rainy day fund for whatever the future might hold.

So many small business ventures fail in the first three years that lenders are not prepared to take risks on them, unless you have a very convincing business plan. The level of risk will also be reflected in the interest rate associated with any loan. Repayments are likely to be a big burden in your profit and loss statements.

Be very wary of borrowing money from friends or relations, no matter how close you are to them. They may give you a very low rate of interest on your repayments, but the problems that often follow if the business falls on hard times can be incredibly stressful. Many long-standing relationships have ended in tears because of small business ventures that have failed. Instead of borrowing from them, another option is to sell a friend or relation a stake in your business. If the business prospers this could be an attractive investment for them. However, if the business fails this can lead to the investor losing all of the money they have put in.

> Many years ago I stupidly loaned money to a relation wanting to buy an antiques business. The business was in very good shape with sound accounts and was making very healthy profits. He had successfully managed this business for some years and consequently I believed he knew the business inside out. What I didn't realise was how inept he would prove to be in comparison with the previous owner. When it came to buying stock and making big financial decisions he was hopeless. The business ultimately failed because of his shortcomings. He wasn't sold a pup and no blame could be attached to the previous owner.
>
> Even if you buy an excellent business and do all the proper groundwork it will still fail if you are not up to the job as an owner. I learned a valuable lesson from this venture. I vowed that I would never again loan money to anyone for a business venture.

Financing your purchase? Checklist

✓ Budget for a purchase price you can afford.
✓ Don't forget to calculate the additional start-up costs involved.
✓ Are you investing capital or taking a loan?
✓ Can you sustain the interest payments on a loan?
✓ Consider carefully before involving friends or family in your investment.
✓ Make sure you understand how to work out a cash flow prediction.
✓ Check your eligibility for grants, e.g. from the government, EU, local authority or related organisation. Information is available from your local Business Link.
✓ Forewarn your investors if your financial situation is changing.

Sole traders, partnerships and limited companies

A shop's accounts may differ greatly depending on who has produced them. When shops are set up as limited companies their accounts must, by law, be verified by a qualified accountant. Most florist shops either have sole trader status or operate as a partnership. They may use an accountant to do the books or they may do the accounts themselves. Many shops have very good detailed accounts. An owner with the right skills will often produce far more detailed information than an accountant would. Some shops will have very few accounts and what they do have may be inaccurate. Unfiled paperwork, stuffed into boxes, is always a bad sign.

Your local Business Link will be able to provide details about limited companies, partnerships and working as a sole trader.

Using an accountant

Many owners do not use an accountant on a regular basis, except perhaps for year-end accounting. They want the sort of bang up-to-date management information that only they can provide. If you employ an accountant it will be some time before you know how the business has performed over a given period. This can be inconvenient. For example, you will need to examine your stock purchase ratios in relation to your sales. By the time the accountant provides this information you may find that you have a problem you should have addressed weeks or even months before.

> I devised my own computerised accounting system that I checked on a Sunday morning to know exactly how we had done in the previous week.
>
> We played a little game whereby this information would dictate where we ate Sunday lunch. A good net profit for the week enabled us to have a very good lunch in one of Cambridge's better restaurants. A smaller profit meant we restricted ourselves to a pub lunch and a loss meant eating at home. Fortunately it was very rare that we ate at home on a Sunday.

Whether or not you already have a good knowledge of business and accounting fundamentals I would strongly recommend that you use a qualified accountant to check through three years' worth of accounts for any business you are considering buying. Bear in mind, however, that even this level of checking may not be sufficient. Most accountants do not have the specialised knowledge of the retail florist sector that an experienced owner will have. There are potential problems that an accountant will not find. Consequently I would also recommend using any contacts you may have within the floristry sector to study the accounts with you, respecting the small print of any non-disclosure agreement you may have signed with an agent or broker.

So just what are you looking for when you study the accounts? Firstly you want to know the sales turnover and the real net profit. If these are poor you will probably not want to proceed any further, unless the asking price is very low and you have a broader plan.

Level of sales and profits

I said in chapter 1 that to make a comfortable living from a shop it should be achieving a sales turnover of at least £250,000 a year. However, for many people, the shop is not their sole source of income. Many people can manage on a smaller turnover.

When we bought our first shop in 1995 it had achieved turnover of only £50,000 in the previous year. Because we considered it to be the first step of a longer-term plan, and because I had a well-salaried position, this little shop fully met our objectives. After four years turnover had grown by some 80 per cent. Net profit was around 10 per cent and we sold the shop for 40 per cent more than we paid for it. More importantly though, Liz and I felt we had learned an enormous amount. We had readied ourselves for the purchase of a much larger shop from which we could both make a living.

It is a considerable risk to buy a large shop as your first venture, even if you have the means to do so. It would be essential for the shop to have excellent staff, including a manager capable of taking full responsibility for the day-to-day running of the business. As a new, inexperienced owner you could learn the business from the staff. However, the staff would need to be very competent and totally trustworthy. They would not take kindly to a new and inexperienced owner commenting on the quality of their work and suggesting changes until the owner could demonstrate that they could do it better.

The profit and loss statement will give you the figures for sales, stock costs, general operating expenses and a net profit. You have to dig much deeper to analyse the numbers and work out exactly what you could expect to make from that business.

Checking the costs

One of the most obvious things to check is the real cost of labour. This may be very different from the figure shown in the wages line of the profit and loss account. If the owners are actively working in the business, you need to find out how they are remunerated.

They may pay themselves wages, which will give an accurate reflection of the number of hours they work and a realistic hourly rate. If this is included in the wages total, all well and good. However many owners prefer not to pay themselves a regular wage. They take money from the business as and when they need it. This is referred to as drawings on the company's accounts. Drawings will not usually show up in the accounting information provided.

You must try to establish how many hours a week the proprietors typically put in and then estimate a fair hourly wage for the work they do. This figure should then be added to the general wages costs to produce a more accurate representation of total labour costs. Then you can examine what impact this has on the net profit.

For example, the profit and loss account of a shop might show a net profit of £40,000. You discover that the two owners are working in the shop full time. Their roles would typically earn each of them approximately £15,000 per annum, which reduces the real net profit to just £10,000.

Many purchasers don't make the necessary checks on wage costs and can end up in a situation where they have effectively bought themselves a job, rather than a truly profitable business. You should ask for detailed information about each person employed, their hourly wage and the number of hours worked per week. Calculate the true total labour cost, including the employer's National Insurance contributions, and then compare this with the figures in the profit and loss statements.

Vendors and agents will often quote a figure for 'add-backs'. These are expenses that the owners choose to put through the books, often for tax reasons, but which a new owner would not perceive to be real costs. They might include private motoring, home computing, personal stationery and postage, cleaning materials, refreshments, home utility bills, private telephone costs and a host of other things. Many of these items are quite legitimate business expenses. For example, the owner might spend an average of two days a week at home working on shop administration. It is only fair that a proportion of the household bills for heat, light and rates, etc., should appear in the shop accounts.

What is much more dubious is when figures for depreciation of capital items, such as delivery vehicles, appear in the profit and loss statement classed as amounts that should be added back into the net profits. Depreciation of vehicles is a real cost and should be considered as part of the true costs of the business. Even though the vehicles may already be bought and paid for, a business should always be making provision for their reduced worth and the need to fund replacement vehicles in the future.

Checking the costs? Checklist

✓ Are you confident you know the real costs of the business you are buying?

✓ Make sure you understand the major parts of a profit and loss statement: sales figures, direct costs, profit, depreciation.

✓ Check the total costs of the wage bill, including the proprietors' likely salary.

✓ Find out what you can about the extent of drawings from the company account.

✓ Examine the accounts carefully for illegitimate 'add-backs'.

Inspecting the paperwork

To verify the figures shown in the accounts ask for copies of the VAT returns to satisfy yourself that they correspond. Also ask to see copies of bank statements, debtors' and creditors' lists and supplier invoices. You need to satisfy yourself that these do correspond with the accounts.

Owners must keep detailed records for a period of at least six years to comply with tax regulations. This is because they may be subject to an inspection by the Inland Revenue or Customs & Excise at any time. Much of my loft space is taken up with boxes of paperwork relating to all the incomings and outgoings of the shops that we have owned. They proved invaluable some years ago when we had a VAT inspection.

Two officials from Customs & Excise spent the best part of a day in my office randomly checking all sorts of paperwork. They were very appreciative that everything was correctly filed and that I could quickly find everything they asked for. I suspect that the tone of their visit would have been much less friendly if I had spent ages scrabbling through piles of unsorted paperwork. They examined sales records that I had generated myself, and the supplier invoices for stock and services supplied. They also wanted to check all the invoices and statements from the provider of our relay service.

I have been almost disappointed that each time we put a shop up for sale no prospective purchaser has ever asked to check the veracity of our records. I have always kept the sort of detailed records that I would expect any buyer to want to see. I would have been pleased to be able to prove that all the paperwork did exist. Not only would it have proved the accuracy of the figures in the accounts but it would also have made all the effort seem worthwhile!

It is important to check that the figures relating to relay transactions have been correctly applied to the accounts. We have been members of both Teleflorist and Interflora. They both supplied detailed invoices, statements and accounting guidelines.

Interflora provides very detailed guidance in a Finance Handbook that is issued to all their members. If the instructions are not correctly followed then it is quite possible for the accounts to be completely distorted. You may not know this if you take over a business and continue to use the same accounting methods as the previous owner, in which case you could receive a terrible shock when the VAT inspector pays a visit.

Gross profits and mark-ups

The gross profit figure also needs examination to get a picture of what sort of mark-up the owners have been applying and what sort of wastage of stock is the norm. The mark-up on the wholesale purchase of stock typically applied by shop owners is a multiplier of approximately 2.5. Most florists will take the price per stem, net of VAT, that they pay their wholesaler. This is trebled to arrive at a retail price that includes VAT. If you calculate the VAT implications, this works out to a real multiplier of 2.55.

Take an example of a stem bought from a wholesaler for £1 plus VAT. This would typically be sold in a shop for £3 including VAT. You can reclaim the 17.5p VAT you paid the wholesaler. The 44.5p in VAT that your customer paid belongs to Customs & Excise. After the VAT calculations you are left with a real margin of £1.55p.

Obviously this does not mean that gross sales should work out at 2.55 times the stock costs, because account has to be taken of wastage. Other items such as sundries, giftware, etc., usually need different multipliers applied to them. After stripping out the VAT and adjusting for relay orders it is more realistic for total sales to be approximately double total purchases.

A typical and realistic situation is a gross profit in relation to sales of between 45 to 55 per cent. This is arrived at by deducting the total cost of all purchases from the total sales, then dividing the result by the total sales. This can change due to many factors. I see shops for sale where the owners are claiming a gross profit of anything between 40 and 60 per cent (and more). A shop in a prime town centre location may have a gross profit that is higher than the average because they can charge premium prices. Conversely their rent and rates are likely to be much higher than average and so their high operating expenses will reduce the net profit.

You need to ask questions about what mark-up has been used and why. If the mark-up has been low it may give new owners the opportunity to increase prices. This could increase the profits but may reduce the volume of sales. The owners may have been forced to use low mark-ups because of fierce local competition. However, there are some shops that under-price because of sheer naïvety. If the mark-up has been higher than average this may be because the customer base is relatively affluent and products are not particularly price sensitive. A florist shop in central London will typically have to apply high mark-ups to compensate for their very high costs for rent, rates and labour, etc.

Claims of high gross profits can be very misleading. The real measure of a business is the true net profit.

Claims of unrecorded sales

One aspect that is difficult, usually impossible, to ascertain is the thorny issue of sales that do not go through the books. Many sellers will claim that lots of cash sales are not rung up on the till. This can never be verified.

A decision on whether or not to make an offer for a shop should always be based on the verifiable accounts of the business, although an assessment of what the owner tells you is always likely to have some impact on the buyer.

If a customer paying for a purchase thrusts £50 in the owner's hand and immediately rushes out of the shop this leaves the owner with a choice to make. Of that £50 some £7.45 VAT will be due to Customs & Excise. Ultimately some £12.76 will be due to the Inland Revenue in terms of income tax and National Insurance contributions when the year-end accounts are filed. Thus the owner has to decide whether to be totally honest and net less than £30 or whether to be opportunistic and pocket the full £50. He or she may be totally honest and want every single transaction to be accurately recorded in the accounts and the tax returns. However, it would be naïve in the extreme to assume that every shop owner does this with every sale.

Tax inspectors are well aware of the norm for each and every type of business they visit. Most owners will know that tax inspectors have guidelines of what to expect. In terms of sales in relation to costs, they will know if an owner is being unreasonably greedy. Some owners will stop bending the rules once they decide to prepare their business for sale. They may *tell* you that they have been taking lots of money that does not go through the till, whereas they might actually have been putting everything through the till. This would make the accounts look as good as possible and maximise the potential asking price for the business.

Assessing the value of a business

I cannot repeat too often that you really must do your homework. Assess the worth of a business by what you observe and can verify for yourself in the accounts. If you go ahead with a purchase you could subsequently realise that sales are better than expected. If you suspect this is because, previously, lots of money failed to find its way to the till, treat this as a bonus. However, if the vendors tell you they have been pocketing lots of money you should be very suspicious. Make your offer based primarily on what you have hard evidence of.

When buying a house it is standard practice to have a solicitor make the appropriate searches. They check for any external factors that may affect the value of the asset in the future. The same concerns apply when purchasing a business. If there are plans to build a by-pass, which may reduce the volume of your passing trade, this could be a big worry. On the other hand, plans to build a large new housing estate nearby could significantly increase your potential customer base in the future.

Let's assume that you have done all your homework as diligently as possible. You have looked at the shop, the stock and the accounts. You have studied the business trends, the customer base, the competition and possible threats and opportunities. You have also assessed the current owners and their staff as best you can. Now you have to decide what sort of offer you might make. Before you can do this you obviously have to think long and hard about what the business is worth to you.

You will need access to sufficient funds to buy the goodwill, the stock, fixtures and fittings and vehicles. You will also need enough for the start-up costs and solicitor's fees, plus sufficient reserves to ensure you have no cash flow problems in the first few months. A certain proportion of the asking price will be for fixtures and fittings. These should be detailed separately. You should check all of those assets to see if you believe the amount asked really does reflect their true worth.

The value of the stock is usually jointly agreed by both the vendor and the purchaser. This is normally accomplished by doing a stock check at the time of completing the sale. This valuation should be based upon the wholesale cost of all of the stock that is deemed to be of good merchantable quality. You would not expect to pay for stock that is clearly old and grubby. If you don't think that you could sell a particular item then don't buy it.

The value of motor vehicles is also usually kept separate from other assets. This is best verified by personally checking the condition and mileage and studying the guide prices for the model. Some of the monthly car price guide periodicals available in any newsagent also include vans. It is also worth checking out *What Van* magazine (www.whatvan.co.uk). In assessing the worth of any vehicles some allowance should be made for any signwriting as impressive graphics on a van will add value. Ask for verification of what the owner paid for the signage and assess its condition. For example, assume the owner paid £10,000 for the van and the guide price is now £5,000. If the owner paid £500 for signage and that signage is still in good condition then it would be reasonable to value it at £250.

But by far the biggest asset of the typical florist shop is the goodwill and the asking price will consist mostly of the cost of goodwill. This is a reflection of the volume of sales that have been built up over the lifetime of the business by virtue of the efforts and the investment made by the owners. This may be related to an earnings multiple or the return on capital employed. The earnings multiple is typically between two and three times what you have assessed the true profit to be. This is after making adjustments to the net profit declared in the accounts for such things as genuine add-backs and owners' wages, etc.

For example, the value of goodwill for a shop that you assess is making a true net profit of £20,000 per annum may be assessed as between £40,000 and £60,000. Whether it is at the upper or lower end of that scale will depend upon the trends shown in the past three years' accounts and the potential for future growth. For a shop that can demonstrate consistent growth in sales, in an improving location, the multiple will be at the high end. A shop that has experienced flat or even declining sales, or which is located in an area experiencing hard times, will merit a low valuation and may represent a high risk at any price.

You might prefer to value a business based upon the return on capital employed. To do this you have to work out the rate of return you want from whatever capital you have to invest. This will obviously be a much higher rate than if you simply invested your money in a bank or building society because the risk is much higher and the returns much less certain.

Typically, purchasers of a florist shop would be looking for a return of some 20 per cent on the capital invested, before interest and tax. If you estimate that the grand total of the capital you need to invest is £100,000 then you might seek an annual net profit of circa £20,000 to justify this.

Of course the real worth of any business is what someone is prepared to pay for it. Any valuation methods similar to those described will go out of the window if the purchaser wants the business badly enough. I have known many people in the floristry sector purchase a particular shop primarily because they are buying into a whole new way of life. Even though the asking price may be high, the financial returns low, and the hours long and hard, many people are so enthusiastic about the prospect of owning and working in their own florist shop that they are prepared to pay far more than a hard-headed businessman would for a business.

Assessing the value of a business? Checklist

✓ Do not let your heart rule your head when assessing the value of a business, however much you think you want it.

✓ Satisfy yourself that the business accounts are correct.

✓ Employ a solicitor to do a local search.

✓ Make sure you have a realistic idea of the worth of the business.

✓ Consider the value of stock, fixtures and fittings, vehicles, start-up costs, solicitor's fees, etc.

✓ Do not purchase anything from the vendor that you will not be able to use or sell.

✓ Make sure you have sufficient reserves to cover the first few months of trading.

✓ Make an accurate calculation of the value of the business's goodwill.

Making an offer

Having worked out what you believe is the true worth of the business you should set an upper limit on what you are prepared to pay, then assess what your opening offer should be. If you genuinely believe the shop has been undervalued and there are lots of people interested, a low offer might mean you run the risk of missing the boat. Do not allow yourself to be carried away by what the agent and the vendor tell you about the level of interest but try to verify it. How long has the business been on the market and what are the reasons for the owners selling?

An offer that is too low can alienate the owner and this may become a problem at a later stage. If the owner reluctantly accepts a low offer they may strike a much harder bargain when you come to agree the valuation of stock and vehicles. It is always best to conduct negotiations in such a way that an amicable relationship is forged with the vendors. They can be an enormous help with the many questions you will still have after the purchase is concluded. These may relate to customer requirements, regular annual orders, invoicing of account customers and historical information on peak periods.

While some shops sell at the full asking price, some eventually sell for less than half the original price. I have looked at shops in poor locations, with terrible accounts and no discernible potential. Having dismissed them as 'unsaleable' I have been staggered to discover that people have bought them at the asking price. From talking to other owners over the years I estimate that the average price actually achieved by shops for sale is around 85 per cent of the original asking price, although I have no hard evidence of this. An initial offer could be as low as 75 per cent of the asking price. However, this clearly depends upon what you calculate to be the true worth of the business, the level of interest by other prospective purchasers and how desirable the shop is to you personally.

If prospective purchasers are queuing up for viewings, and the vendor has a genuine reason for a quick sale, a higher offer might be justified. You want to avoid missing out on a really good opportunity but you must resist being carried away by misplaced optimism. Estate agents love viewers who fall madly in love with a house. They are so keen that they readily believe that it is sure to sell quickly. They offer the full asking price and it is accepted. The agent returns to the office chuckling at their naïvety. Be sure you do not make this mistake with a shop.

> When we acquired Biggs Florist in Cambridge the asking price was reasonable but there were many other factors that influenced us to make an offer. Various different factors played a part in our decision to buy. The shop had enormous potential and we were very impressed by the staff. The books were good and access was easy, with plenty of parking.
>
> We sold the shop because of Liz's illness. With good verifiable accounts and solid growth we had prospective buyers competing with each other. A quick sale for the full asking price was easy to achieve and we could almost certainly have achieved a higher sale figure. However, our main motivation was for a quick sale because of the speed at which Liz's health was deteriorating.

Having agreed a price the agent will want a deposit of up to 10 per cent to show your commitment to proceeding with the purchase. Solicitors acting for each party will then need to finalise the contract of sale. They will handle all the necessary legal work relating to the leasehold or freehold. Whether you take out a new lease, or have the balance of an existing lease assigned to you, will affect the length of time the whole transaction will take. An assignment of an existing lease is usually much quicker to arrange. You will have to assess the benefits of this against the reduced security of tenure in the future.

I cannot stress enough that the key thing is to do your homework as thoroughly as possible. Once you have signed on the dotted line and the sale is completed there is no turning back.

Making an offer? Checklist

✓ Be clear about the worth and desirability of the business to you personally.

✓ Keep a cool head.

✓ Maintain good relations with the vendors – their help will be invaluable later.

3 Relay services

This chapter looks at:

- The need for a relay service
- The threats to relay services
- The benefits of the established relay organisations
- Quality and standards
- Joining a relay service
- Monitoring your performance
- Accounting information
- The profitability of relay orders

A relay service enables a florist shop to take an order from a customer for delivery to an address that is outside the delivery area for that shop. The delivery address may be twenty miles away or it might be on the other side of the world. The order is relayed by the sending florist, who makes the sale to the customer. It is then received by an executing florist, who will fulfil the order and deliver it to the recipient.

The need for a relay service

A typical florist shop will receive many orders for flowers and associated products to be delivered outside the local area and so it is essential to have some means of accepting and fulfilling such orders.

It is possible for a shop to avoid the costs involved in membership of one of the reputable relay organisations but I believe this is a very false economy. Some shops will simply find a florist in the recipient's area and phone that florist to place an order, as if they were just another customer. There are a number of problems with doing this, however, both in terms of quality and finance.

The sender may simply deduct an amount from the order value they give to the executing florist, to give themselves a profit margin. This can represent a very poor deal to both the sending florist and the customer. Unless the sending florist receives some sort of VAT receipt from the executing florist they cannot legitimately reclaim the VAT on the relayed order. However, they will be liable to pay VAT on the sale they have made to the customer.

Often the sender finds it difficult to obtain a proper VAT receipt. Thus either the profit margin will be very small or the customer will get a bad deal, as the VAT is effectively being paid twice. Many florists are reluctant to accept such orders from another florist. They will be concerned about what the customer has paid and the likelihood of a future complaint relating to poor value. If the customer pays a total of £35 and then sees that what was actually delivered to the recipient looks more like £20 worth, they will understandably be very unhappy. Some florists will work on the assumption that the customer will not see what is delivered but this is a risky assumption and is often wrong.

Some florists will not relay orders to another florist but arrange instead for the product to be made up and mailed to the recipient. The quality and appearance of the product will both suffer before they finally reach the recipient.

I have frequently delivered flowers to a recipient at the same time as a courier service has delivered boxed flowers to the same person. I always took great pleasure from the reaction of the recipient as I handed them a beautiful bouquet compared with the muted reaction they gave to the box from the courier.

My recommendation is to use a reputable, established relay service such as Interflora, Teleflorist or Flowergram.

The threats to relay services

Apart from the problems of florists who choose to deal directly with another florist there are also a number of very dubious organisations operating in the relay sector. Typically they will take telephone orders directly from customers and then relay this order to any florist they can find in the recipient's area who is prepared to deliver a product for them.

Many of these organisations are making an extortionate profit by passing on only a small fraction of the order value to the executing florist. They may, for example, take an order for £50 and pass only half of this on to the executing florist, which means the customer receives very poor value for their money.

Often the executing florist is duped by these organisations as they pose as customers and the first the executor knows of any problem is when they receive a complaint about poor value. This leaves the executor in a quandary over what to do, as the sending organisation usually does not want to be involved. Some florists decide to deliver more flowers as an apology and so through no fault of their own they sustain a loss while the sender pockets a fat profit just for making a phone call.

Using a reputable relay service means that there is fair and acknowledged distribution of the money paid by the customer. Some of the proceeds go to the sending florist who has made the sale, some go the relay service as payment for the service they provide and the bulk goes to the executing florist who has to make up and deliver the order to the recipient.

A new problem for relay organisations is that, with access to modern IT systems, many customers are simply bypassing them. They use the Internet or telephone directory services to find a florist shop in the recipient's area. This enables them to contact the florist direct and cut out any intermediary. A shop receiving a relay order will receive approximately two-thirds of the price paid by the customer. Consequently their profit margin on relay orders can be very small or even non-existent. Many customers realise that if they deal direct they can get much better value. As people grow more and more accustomed to using the Internet to purchase all sorts of products and services directly, this problem is only likely to get worse for agencies acting as intermediaries.

Over the past two years the suppliers of boxed flowers have become a significant new competitor. This used to be a niche market, originated by some growers in the Channel Islands, but it was adopted by the major supermarkets. Today this market is served by the likes of Tesco, Marks and Spencer, Debenhams, Boots, Next, John Lewis, the Post Office, Clinton Cards, Stringfellows and even Jane Packer. Their biggest problem lies in correctly delivering an attractive product that makes an immediate and positive impact on the recipient. Many of these products meet with a very unenthusiastic response. The impact that can be made by a local florist delivering a fresh product, with instant visual appeal, is far more impressive.

The benefits of the established relay organisations

I must state straight away that my views on established relay organisations are based only on my personal experience. Each of the different organisations has its own scales of charges for joining fees, membership fees, orders relayed and other services. These services include IT, directories, marketing materials, accessories and sundries, etc.

The different organisations have their own standards for membership that will enable them to determine whether a member shop fulfils their criteria. These criteria cover shop appearance, the availability and quality of a range of flowers, quality of make-up work and customer service, among other things.

My personal experience is that by far the most demanding standards are those set by Interflora. To join Interflora you have to meet the necessary criteria and pass a demanding inspection of the shop as a whole, the quality of the stock and the make-up work. There is then an ongoing requirement to maintain those standards and there are severe penalties for anyone consistently failing to come up to standard, which can and do result in expulsions.

Other organisations have less stringent checks and processes. From my observation they are more concerned with signing up as many members as possible. They focus much more on maximising order volumes and the revenues deriving from membership fees, orders and other services.

Interflora membership comes at a cost, with a monthly membership fee of £90* compared with, say, Teleflorist's annual membership fee of £90*. However, the combination of Interflora order volumes, high order values, and relatively low costs per order for the extensive central clearing house services, still makes this attractive for most members.

Interflora is effectively owned by its members, although at present there are plans being advanced for incorporation. If Interflora is to compete with the big supermarkets like Tesco and Sainsbury, with their wealth of data about their customer base, they will need millions of pounds of new investment in marketing and IT. Raising this investment money would involve the members selling much of their rights to a venture capitalist. This would have to be approved by at least 75 per cent of the membership. At the time of writing Interflora is battling an action group, formed by some of their members, who believe that the board of directors are undervaluing the organisation for their own financial gain.

Teleflorist make much of the number of member shops they have but Interflora is by far the best-known brand name and it has become a byword for sending flowers. Teleflorist have some 2,500 members in the UK

*Prices at Spring 2005

against the 1,800 Interflora members. However, the difference in order volumes still makes Interflora very much the dominant player.

We were members of both Teleflorist and Interflora, at various times. We found that being an Interflora member massively increased our order volumes. When we were Teleflorist members customers would ask us daily whether we handled Interflora orders, usually meaning simply, 'Will you take an order for flowers to be delivered somewhere else?' rather than a request for a named service. As an Interflora member I have never known a customer enquire whether we handled Teleflorist orders. Interflora's name has, happily for them, become the generic byword for the service they provide.

While Interflora are relatively cautious and protective about their sales channels, other relay services are keen to capture all the orders they possibly can. Teleflorist allow just about anyone with a website to be an affiliate who can receive orders. These are then routed to Teleflorist in return for a commission of 8 per cent of the order value. Flowergram are a much smaller organisation. Their prices are lower and so are the fees involved. Their current membership fees are around £100 per year and their levy for the provision of clearing house services is only 3.99 per cent*. The conditions for joining Flowergram are much less stringent, but their order volumes are much smaller than Interflora and Teleflorist. However, they claim that order volumes are currently climbing by some 13 per cent per year while Interflora admit their volumes are falling.

Quality and standards

All of the different organisations will help their members to keep up to date with current design trends and to make products in accordance with the current product range. We attended many Interflora meetings and conferences over the years. Some of these were general meetings to listen to presentations and discuss matters relating to all aspects of the business. Some were focused specifically on how to make all of the products in a new range. Some were solely for the owners and proprietors of member shops to discuss business issues. Each year there is a members' conference that addresses all the issues, concerns and future plans over a full weekend. These include open forums, presentations and working groups, including a formal gala dinner.

*Prices at Spring 2005

We found that to make the most of our membership we had to make the effort to attend just about all the meetings and conferences. One disappointment was that attendance at meetings was not compulsory. Consequently we found that although we were regularly meeting certain members, and forming excellent working relationships and lasting friendships with them, there were some members who never seemed to attend. We found it was the most successful shops that were well represented at meetings while the people who needed help and guidance most were absent. Consideration is being given to making it compulsory for every shop to attend a certain number of meetings every year.

Interflora have very strict standards for the content, value and appearance of each product delivered. All of this is specified in a workbook that shows just how the finished product should look. Any customer complaint is treated very seriously and fully investigated. The content of each and every order has to be costed and quantified. This includes the flowers, which are costed by stem, the labour involved in making the product, accessories, message cards, care guides, flower food and administration, etc. This means that if a complaint relates to poor value, the member can double-check and justify the cost of what they have made and supplied.

Joining a relay service

In the UK a florist shop may be a member of only one relay service. As an Interflora member we received many overtures from other relay services who assured us that if we signed up with them it would not jeopardise our Interflora membership. However, Interflora regularly warn their members against this and anyway we had such a large volume of business through Interflora that we would not have wanted to do anything that might put this at risk.

In the US it is common for a shop to belong to multiple relay services. We looked at one shop for sale in Tampa that had five different computer systems for the five different relay services it belonged to. I believe that the combined costs and potential profitability of belonging to multiple services do not stand up to close scrutiny. Many shops underestimate the profitability of outgoing orders and overestimate the profitability of incoming orders they have to execute.

In my opinion the most important thing is to use one reliable, good quality service that will enable you to send outgoing orders to just about anywhere in the world. This should be a profitable part of the business and any florist shop has to be able to offer this sort of service to any customer. Apart from the financial considerations it would be very embarrassing to have to tell a customer that you can only handle local orders.

There are many businesses springing up that claim to provide a low cost, high return service to a florist that will not affect their membership of any other relay service. I would strongly advise that you resist the approaches of anyone other than an established relay service that can demonstrate it has the infrastructure in place to handle millions of orders being relayed between thousands of member florists.

If you take over a shop that is already a member of a relay service, and you wish to continue membership, you will have to reapply as a new owner. The previous owners will have to resign and at that point you can apply for new membership. This is not usually a problem with most relay service operators, provided you meet the criteria and pay the fees involved. Interflora will want reassurance that the existing staff will be retained by any new owners.

Usually your membership of a relay service will not provide you with a guaranteed region. If another florist in your area applies for membership this will usually be granted, if they meet the necessary criteria. If your shop has built up a customer base in the local area and has provided a good level of orders to that relay service, this can seem very unfair. Part of Interflora's plans for incorporation include some form of area protection for their existing members.

Monitoring your performance

An aspect of Interflora membership that I particularly liked was that together with all the detailed accounting information they provided at the end of the month, each shop also receives a page of statistics showing how they are performing in relation to other members. These statistics show your shop's incoming and outgoing order volumes for the month and compare them with the same month in the previous year. Year to date volumes and comparisons are also made. The average value of each order you send is compared with all other shops and also with all the other sales channels such as central telesales and the Interflora website, etc.

These monthly statistics also show your shop's position in relation to all the member shops across the UK and to the other shops in your region of the country. These figures reflect the total value of all the orders your shop sends through the Interflora system. It is invaluable to know how you are performing in comparison to your fellow members. I would recommend anyone planning to buy a shop that is an Interflora member to ask to see these statistics for the past couple of years. It is an excellent indicator of how well the shop is doing and whether the trends are improving or declining.

> When we took over the shop in Cambridge we found that we were ranked 154 out of a total of 2,145 shops nationwide and 25 out of the 178 members in the East Anglia region. We then set about climbing the ladder and motivated the staff with informal bonus schemes. We gave all our staff an objective to beat the average value per order and we soon found that the girls were working hard to drive up order values. They learned how best to sell a larger bouquet or arrangement and to offer add-ons, such as chocolates, teddy bears and balloons. Everyone took great satisfaction as we climbed up to number 59 nationwide and number 7 in East Anglia.

Accounting information

Apart from these monthly statistics each member is sent detailed accounting information showing each and every order that your shop has sent and received. The details are clearly listed for both UK and overseas orders so that the VAT is correctly applied. We found that both Teleflorist and Interflora provided detailed guidance on how to apply all these details to your shop accounts and I can particularly recommend the finance handbook provided by Interflora.

Different shops may apply the relay financials to their accounts in different ways but the key thing is to ensure that the sales and costs can be clearly identified and the correct amount of VAT is paid. When we had a VAT inspection I found that the inspectors concentrated mostly on the paperwork relating to relay orders, presumably as this is the area where florists are most likely to get confused.

It is standard practice for a relay service to retain a proportion of the proceeds due to a new member by way of a deposit. The size of this deposit can vary depending upon the volume of orders and may range from a few hundred pounds for a small shop to a much greater sum for a large shop. This retained deposit provides protection for the relay service if a member ceases trading or fails to pay its dues. The deposit is returned to the member once it leaves the service and all the final transactions have been accounted for and all the final payments have been settled.

The profitability of relay orders

From studying the accounting information and the breakdown of the amount paid by a customer, an owner can ascertain just how profitable or otherwise their relay orders are.

Depending on the relay service used, the proportion of the order value that is retained by the sender is typically 25 per cent of the total. About 67 per cent goes to the executing florist whilst the central relay service will keep approximately 8 per cent.

Many shops assume that incoming orders are more profitable than outgoing orders but in fact the reverse is true. A study of the Yellow Pages shows many businesses that take orders over the phone or the Internet that they relay on to an executing florist. Many of these businesses give the impression of being a local florist shop whereas they are simply a telesales operation and do not provide flowers in any shape or form themselves. Some of these advertisers are florist shops that place adverts in Yellow Pages directories in other regions and capture many orders from the local florists there.

A figure of 25 per cent for the sender of an order may not sound much but there are many high value orders placed these days. We once took an order from a local business wanting to send a total of 27 bouquets to employees of another company in the US. The very next call was someone placing an order of over £350 for a funeral in the north west.

However, many florists question the profitability of their incoming orders. Once the true costs of stock, labour, accessories, administration, delivery and relay service membership are taken in to account it may be that the real net profit is either very small or non-existent. Interflora's view on incoming orders is that although each individual order may not make a real net profit, it will make a valuable contribution to the costs of the business. If you do not accept incoming orders, you will not have the opportunity to reduce other general overheads accordingly. You still have to pay the same amounts for rent, rates, water, electricity and insurance. Incoming orders *do* make a positive contribution to the overall profitability of the business.

You may take the view that you want to be able to send orders but do not want to receive incoming relay orders. This has become a real problem for some shops in high rent areas such as central London. Many of these have found that the fixed starting prices publicised by their relay service provider mean they lose money on most incoming orders. Trying to make a profit from an order for a £20 gift-wrapped bouquet, for delivery in Mayfair, is out of the question. Many shops in this situation have reluctantly decided that they have to resign their relay membership and seek alternative methods to send their outgoing orders.

Choosing a relay service? Checklist

✓ Use only an established and trustworthy relay service.
✓ Concentrate on maximising your outgoing orders.
✓ Accept that incoming orders are less profitable but still worthwhile.

4 Buying stock

This chapter looks at:

- Where to buy stock
- Cooperative ventures
- Conditioning the stock
- Wastage of stock

- Mark-ups and pricing
- Marking up non-floral products
- Peak periods
- Giving products away

Buying stock is a crucial aspect of the retail floristry trade and one over which an owner has a great deal of influence. You may feel you have little flexibility for cutting the costs of many of the general operating expenses of the shop. However you can have an enormous impact on what you spend on stock, how you look after it and what price you sell it for.

Liz did most of the buying for our shops and when she became ill Jo, the manager, took on the role. They focused on ensuring we bought whatever we needed, from the best suppliers we could find, to fulfil all the orders. While they checked all the stock for quality and vase life, I spent a lot of time on the financial aspects of stock purchasing.

Where to buy stock

Most florists rely mostly on the different wholesale suppliers who visit their shop. Depending on the location, most shops will have a range of Dutch deliverers and other local wholesalers visiting them on a regular basis.

The Dutch normally use a large refrigerated lorry that they fill with fresh flowers, foliage and plants. We used to use suppliers who bought and loaded at the Dutch auctions. They would cross the Channel overnight and call on us and other Cambridge florists early the following morning. Once the different shops in Cambridge had been called on, the wholesaler would venture further afield, spending several days visiting other florists across East Anglia and the south east before heading back to Holland.

They would often have an arrangement whereby they offloaded all their remaining stock to someone at a very low price before leaving the UK.

Often these job lots of stock end up being sold at the side of the road or on a market stall. It can be very frustrating for a florist to be challenged by a customer over why their prices are far higher than those on a market stall. We used to take time to explain to customers that the flowers they bought cheaply in the market had often been on a lorry for several days and had also been rejected by the many florists that the wholesaler had visited. The wholesaler could either throw them away or get whatever price they could for them. There are always people prepared to take someone's old stock if they think they can make an easy profit. But the rule is inescapable: you get what you pay for.

Many of our customers were very interested to hear this sort of thing. It reinforced their decision to buy their flowers from a proper florist shop. It made them more likely to feel that they were buying wisely.

We always found that the local wholesalers provided a good, reliable service but had great difficulty competing with the prices that the Dutch could offer. Most of the local wholesalers that we used regularly were specialists in one particular sector, some in plants, some in accessories and sundries, and some in giftware such as pots and vases.

A constant problem is the way the Dutch price their stock. We found that different shops were charged very different prices. Occasionally we would phone some of our local competitors and share information about what each of us had been charged that day by a particular supplier. Some differential pricing can be justified because a large shop, consistently buying large volumes, can expect to receive some sort of volume discount. However, some pricing can be purely opportunistic. Hard-nosed hagglers can pay significantly less than pleasant, friendly florists who accept whatever price they are charged.

One of the Dutch wholesalers we used gave us intimate access to their website. We could not only check on their pricing but also find out what they had paid for stock at the Aalsmeer auctions. This supplier also listed the prices by stem on the shelves in the lorry. This made it easy for florists to know what the current prices were and then decide whether or not to buy.

Other suppliers would fax us their current price list the day before calling so we could plan our purchases ahead. This was a great help and solved the problem of what to do when a wholesaler called and you felt some of the prices were too high. If no other supplier is calling that day you might have to buy anyway.

The buying process is usually a difficult balance of gauging prices against quality levels. We found that often a new wholesaler would visit us offering very impressive prices and excellent quality but that unfortunately they could not maintain this over a period of time. Either prices would creep up and/or the quality would dip and you began to suspect they were selling some old stock.

With some suppliers we found that entering into any sort of volume purchasing arrangement was a bad idea. Although the prices dropped, they began to rely on us buying in large volume, and the quality levels would also drop.

Some florists are prepared to get out of bed in the middle of the night and drive to market to buy and collect their stock. If you are experienced enough and you know that you are buying good quality flowers at the best market prices then this can represent huge savings. However, if you are not experienced it is easy to pay over the odds and lose a lot of sleep for very little return. I have always been very impressed by some experienced florists who get up at 3am, drive to New Covent Garden, do all their buying and then unload the flowers at their shop before working a full day. I have to say that we never had that much energy. We were quite happy to have wholesalers delivering just about everything we needed, even if it meant accepting a lower level of profit.

Had Liz and I entered the floristry trade when we were in our twenties or thirties things might have been different. We would have had the drive and the energy to buy regularly at market because we would have been hungry for the extra profit.

Another method of buying is to do it all over the Internet and have stock delivered directly. It might come direct from the markets or even directly from the growers. It is buying stock in much the same way as many people purchase their groceries these days. When we tried to do this we met with a number of problems, usually related to the means of delivery. Delivery is usually made by some sort of generalised delivery business, rather than by anyone who has any specialised knowledge of flowers and their care. Consequently we had problems with deliveries arriving out of shop hours. Some of the stock was delivered in a non-refrigerated lorry and we had difficulties with returning trolleys and containers to suppliers. One supplier charged us a deposit for the trolleys and for each of the buckets delivered to us. We then experienced all sorts of problems with getting these deposits correctly credited back to us when we returned them.

It may be that levels of service for this sort of on-line buying will improve in the future. My advice would be to use this method with great caution, and only after you have checked out all aspects of the delivery process in great detail.

Where to buy stock? Checklist

✓ Investigate local wholesalers for specialist items.
✓ Check on the reliability and competitiveness of wholesalers' prices.
✓ Arrange for wholesalers to supply you with a stock and price list ahead of their visit.
✓ If you have the time and energy, consider going to market yourself.
✓ Use Internet suppliers with caution.

Cooperative ventures

Another means of buying stock is to enter into some form of cooperative venture with other florists. We did try this but I have to admit it was not a success. I will describe how this works only to provide a warning to anyone considering this idea.

We joined a cooperative of independent florists to set up a business that would enable us to buy flowers directly from the Dutch auctions. They would be delivered directly to each member shop in our own refrigerated lorry. The business hired a buyer-driver and leased a lorry. We all entered into it with high hopes of greatly reduced prices and better quality flowers. To make the cooperative work it needed a core of some 25 member shops. This would enable us all to make significant savings if the concept proved to be workable. We were sceptical from the outset but the potential savings of cutting out a wholesaler were so great that we decided to give it a try.

The first deliveries were fraught with problems, mainly due to logistics. We had to work to such tight deadlines. The driver needed to fit in the buying, loading, ferry journeys and delivering to shops covering an area from London to Yorkshire. After the first month things improved a little but there were still many problems. It seemed that we had not been told the whole truth about how many members had committed to the scheme and paid their share of the start-up costs.

It became obvious there were fewer than the 25 members required in the business plan. This meant members were being asked to pay slightly more per stem to make up the shortfall. Some members decided at an early stage that the concept would never work and pulled out. Before long there were more shops pulling out than new members joining and the whole venture collapsed.

It was a shame that this did not work because for a short spell after the initial teething problems it looked as though it might. For a while we were receiving deliveries of excellent quality flowers at the lowest prices we had ever achieved. But the whole venture had only lasted a few months.

When I came to do all the sums after we had pulled out I found that we had still made a small saving when everything was taken into account. However, these figures did not take into account the many meetings we attended and the time wasted in trying to manage the problems we experienced. So we took the view that although it had been an interesting exercise, which had not actually lost us any money, we would never venture into a similar scheme ever again.

I am told by some wholesalers and shop owners that similar schemes have been tried before but all have failed, usually because of the problems involved in getting enough shops signed up and sufficiently committed to making it work.

Conditioning the stock

Probably the least popular job in a florist shop is conditioning the stock as it arrives in the shop. This involves stripping off the leaves and thorns, cutting stems and getting the flowers into water. Although this is a very important task it is usually considered to be very boring work and it is also extremely tiring.

It is also very important to regularly clean all the buckets and vases with bleach and water. Then they should be thoroughly rinsed out with fresh water. If this is not done, bacteria can rapidly kill off your stock.

I know of one shop where the new owner asked his florists what he could do to help out. They replied that bleaching the vases in the shop was

always a great help to them. At the end of the day, after all the staff had
left, he went round the shop pouring neat bleach into each and every vase.
When the florists arrived the following morning they found all the stock in
the shop had died overnight!

As part of the conditioning work we would randomly check the number of
stems in each wrap or bunch of flowers. Often we found that certain wraps
were all one stem short. If you are getting only 19 stems in each wrap of red
roses at Valentine's Day instead of the full 20, this can represent a significant financial loss. Whenever we challenged a supplier about shortages
they would claim that it was the automated machinery they used which
was at fault. This might sometimes be true but occasionally we suspected
that shortages were not accidental.

We realised that our florists hated conditioning work and so we
employed a Saturday girl to process the big delivery we received early each
Saturday morning. We also hired a driver who could do conditioning work
when not actually delivering. The problem with this was that drivers do
not feel hugely motivated to do this sort of work. They are unlikely to
hurry back to the shop after their last delivery of the day if they know that
conditioning work is waiting for them.

My complete lack of floristry skills meant that conditioning was just
about the only task I could fulfil that involved handing flowers. Actually,
I quite enjoyed conditioning flowers early on a Saturday morning while
chatting to Liz as she got on with the creative work. This may be a poor
reflection on my intellectual capabilities but I think conditioning is a bit
like painting walls at home. It is boring, but sometimes it is nice to do a job
that allows you to think about something completely different from the
task in hand.

One of the best investments we ever made was to have a Chrysal dosing
unit plumbed in. This meant we could use a separate tap to deliver a consistent
measured dosage of preservative into each bucket or vase. We believed
that this extended the vase life of the stock by some two or three days.

Establish a routine for getting all the menial, but still important, jobs
done on a regular basis. These include changing the water in all vases and
buckets, watering plants and ensuring that everything is priced. Check
that there is no old stock slowly rotting away in a corner of your cold room.
Not only will this stink but it also gives off ethylene gas that harms the
stock in the immediate vicinity. Most florists know that this gas also

emanates from various types of fruit and it is a real problem for greengrocers who sell both fruit and flowers.

The ideal temperature for a cold room is generally reckoned to be between 4°–7° C. Often a cold room without full cladding or with an underpowered chiller unit will not be able to get down to these levels. However, as long as it keeps the temperature well below that in the shop it will still be a big help in prolonging flower life.

Conditioning the stock? Checklist

✓ Establish a routine.
✓ Strip leaves and thorns, cut stems and put flowers in water.
✓ Clean all buckets and vases with a bleach solution and rinse with fresh water.
✓ Count the stems in each wrap or bunch.
✓ Consider purchasing a conditioning dosing unit.
✓ Discard old stock promptly.
✓ Maintain room temperature.

Wastage of stock

Stock that is deemed to be of poor quality once it is unwrapped should be put aside. Inform the supplier and either have the stock replaced, if the wholesaler is still in the locality, or have a credit applied to their next invoice. As long as you can demonstrate that the stock was not of merchantable quality then you should never have a problem in obtaining a credit. If you do then you probably will not want to continue using that particular supplier unless you absolutely have to.

We found that in the early days of using a new supplier they would want us to keep any problem stock. They would want to see for themselves that our complaints really were justified. Once suppliers realised that all our complaints were fair and reasonable their trust in us increased. Then they would no longer require us to keep problem stock.

We kept a wastage log for anything we could not use. In this we would log all the details – the date bought, the details of the stock and the supplier, the date it was deemed to be unusable, the reason it was unusable and finally any action taken by the supplier. If it was simply stock that we had failed to sell within a reasonable timescale, this was obviously our problem.

When I first entered the floristry trade I assumed that wastage must be very high but I was pleased to discover that, with good organisation, this was not the case. Stock rotation is obviously essential and staff should use the oldest stock first. When new stock arrives it can be very tempting for florists to pick the very best flowers for whatever they happen to be making. This has to be resisted and a rotation system employed, with stock being used up while it still has a reasonable vase life left.

Open orders, when the customer leaves it up to the florist to select what they put into a bouquet, give you the opportunity to ensure that older stock is used up while it is still of good enough quality.

We found that the Chrysal Professional 2 dosing unit significantly extended flower life. This very effectively delays the flowers opening. Every bouquet or bunch of flowers leaving the shop had flower food attached. This is essential in furthering the life of flowers once they have opened.

Mark-ups and pricing

As previously mentioned the mark-up you apply to the stock purchased is crucially important to your profitability. The usual method for cut flower pricing is to take the wholesale price net of VAT and treble it to arrive at a retail price inclusive of VAT. Thus when the VAT implications are calculated this represents a real mark-up of 2.55 and this will be further reduced by unavoidable wastage.

As the mark-up multiplier used is the decision of the owner there can be wide variations. A shop in an expensive area with an affluent customer base may use a higher multiplier. A shop with lots of local competition, perhaps selling a large volume of cut flowers requiring no make-up work, may be able to use a much smaller mark-up.

Now that I no longer own a shop I have to confess that I occasionally buy cut flowers from the local Tesco and must admit they do represent incredible value. Just a few pounds can buy me a good selection that will often last for three to four weeks, if I make the effort to look after them. I try to change the water regularly, re-cut the stems and use flower food. Having told so many customers over the years to always use a proper florist, instead of a supermarket, I do feel a little disingenuous doing this.

The order sheet for each and every order should have the flower content listed and costed in case of complaint. This is not always possible for very urgent orders, however. When a customer dashes in demanding instant service because his car is on a double yellow line outside you have to act accordingly. Customers in a hurry are not impressed by the florist selecting each and every stem, listing them carefully and adding up the cost. Sometimes a £20 gift wrap has to be produced in not much more than a minute or two. However, an experienced florist knows what £20 worth looks like and can quickly make something appropriate.

Relay orders, however, should certainly be properly costed and detailed. A reputable relay service like Interflora will usually insist upon this.

The value of the flowers included in each made-up product should never be revealed to the customer. Occasionally in the event of complaint it may be necessary to reveal this to Trading Standards. Nevertheless, some customers expect that a £30 bouquet will have £30 worth of flowers in it. It can be very frustrating trying to explain that you have to pay for your rent, rates, staff, electricity, etc.

The mark-up multiplier used may vary at peak periods. Around Valentine's Day you may decide that if you use the normal multiplier for red roses they will appear extortionately expensive. Florists are open to very close scrutiny by the media at such times. You can probably use a smaller multiplier because the greatly increased volume of sales will still enable you to make a good profit.

At peak times such as Valentine's Day it is also a good idea to let customers know just why prices are high. I used to provide a pile of one-page handouts on the shop counter explaining why our prices were higher than usual in Valentine's week. It explained that at peak times all florists need to buy huge volumes of flowers. Nearly all of this stock is bought by wholesalers at an auction. If all of the people attending any auction are absolutely determined to buy huge quantities of whatever is being sold then they cannot expect to pay anything other than premium prices.

This handout also explained that the roses we were selling were typically long stemmed, best grade, Grand Prix roses that had been properly conditioned. Comments in the media about corner shops selling a dozen red roses for less than £10 on Valentine's Day absolutely infuriated me. It is like asking a Jaguar dealer why the car in his showroom is priced at £45,000 when you know where you can get a car for £500.

You need to display prominently the current prices of your cut flowers, perhaps on a whiteboard or blackboard. A simple solution is to use little blackboard picks in each vase or bucket. These enable you to state both the flower name and the price per stem. Most customers do not know the names of flowers and may be embarrassed to ask. They like to look around and then state confidently what they want, using the correct names.

Mark-ups and pricing? Checklist

✓ Establish a reliable multiplier for everyday sales and be prepared to adapt it during peak periods.

✓ Display current prices of cut flowers prominently.

Marking up non-floral products

Mark-ups for giftware and add-ons are often lower than for fresh flowers. Many wholesalers who supply pots and glassware supply products that already have a retail price sticker on each item. This is normally double the wholesale price. Balloons that can be bought for less than a pound will retail for £4 when filled with helium and attached to a bouquet.

Many florists refuse to sell sundries such as baskets, oasis, wire, ribbon, cellophane and message cards. They assume that anyone wanting these items will be an amateur florist or a flower arranger, and therefore effectively a competitor. Some florists do sell these items but only at a very high mark-up. Others take the view that they will cooperate with such customers for the fresh flower sales they might also make to them.

Some florists actively cooperate with local groups of flower arrangers and college floristry courses. They might offer them a discount on both flowers and sundries. This is a decision best made by individual shop owners based on their local situation.

There is certainly a risk in selling cards and/or envelopes that carry your shop name or your relay service name. Many florists can tell stories related to this. A typical example is a complaint from the recipient of some flowers. When investigated, it turns out that only the message card had been bought at the shop. An amateur florist had actually been responsible for the flowers and their make-up.

Peak periods

Planning for peak periods is crucially important. Most shops will make the majority of their annual profits over Christmas, Valentine's Day and Mother's Day. Order too much stock and wastage can be enormous. Order too little and you suffer the frustration of turning customers away.

I can remember when our main deliveries of stock arrived in the run-up to Valentine's Day and Mother's Day. The whole of the shop – the cold room, the store rooms and the sheds at the rear of the shop – would be jam packed with new stock. There were flowers, vases, buckets and baskets everywhere. This was the only time I ever saw Liz look really nervous. It was hard for her to imagine just how we were going to sell it all. She was always anxious that she had got her calculations wrong and had bought far too much.

Every time we got to the end of Valentine's Day and Mother's Day, however, the shop would be as empty as if we had been invaded by a plague of locusts. Despite Liz's fears that one day we would come unstuck it never happened. However, if we had ever woken up to six inches of snow on the morning of Valentine's Day then I'm sure it would have been a disaster.

Liz would put lots of effort into planning this special buying. Usually I did any work that related to numbers and admin but this was different. Before each peak period I would see her surrounded by paperwork from her history files, tapping away on the calculator. She would examine the previous year's invoices in great detail. She studied the stem counts, exactly what had been ordered and what she had paid for it.

After each peak period we would sit down for a debriefing and make notes that went into our history file. These covered what sold easily, what didn't, what labour we had used, what worked well and what didn't. We found these peak period history files absolutely invaluable. Although we never really felt like writing notes directly after such an exhausting period, we forced ourselves to do it. We knew just how much we would regret it the following year if we hadn't made the effort.

The assumption we worked on for Christmas and Mother's Day was that, in comparison with the previous year, trade would be up by whatever was the average for the current year as a whole. However, calculating Valentine's Day is much more complex than that.

So what assumptions can you make if you are taking over a new shop and you do not have any historical data to help your planning? I have gone back through the sales records for all the years that we owned a shop and calculated how big an increase we experienced in the peak period weeks, over and above an average week.

Valentine's Day was always our busiest time of the year. On average the sales for the week leading up to it were 235 per cent more than for a normal week. Mother's Day was always our second busiest week of the year with sales up 145 per cent above the norm. Many florists find that flower buying for Mother's Day has actually decreased in recent years. This seems to be because of the many alternative gifts and treats that are now promoted. A long gap between Valentine's Day and Mother's Day is generally considered to be good news. A lot of people who buy flowers for the first occasion will look for an alternative gift if the second occasion comes soon after.

We never found Christmas anything like as challenging as these two peak periods and average sales in the two weeks prior to the big day would only be 63 per cent above average.

The volume of trade on Valentine's Day will depend mostly upon the day of the week that the 14th happens to fall on, and also upon the weather. For almost all florists, Valentine's Day falling on a weekend is bad news. If it falls on a Friday, sales could be up 10 per cent on the overall Valentine's average. However, if it falls on a Saturday sales can be down by some 10–15 per cent.

Fortunately we never experienced Valentine's Day falling on a Sunday. Those who have tell me it is awful. Orders that would usually be delivered to a recipient at their place of work will be lost. For various reasons, if Valentine's Day falls on a weekend, many senders will not want a delivery made to the recipient's home address.

At a weekend many people will prefer to take their partner out for a meal or they will shop for an alternative gift. Some central London florists who rely almost entirely on commuter trade do not even open for Valentine's Day if it falls on a weekend. Friday is generally thought to be the best day, perhaps because people know they will be in for a difficult weekend if they forget to buy flowers!

The weather also has a big impact. A bright sunny day is much more likely to promote a feeling of well-being and generosity. A heavy snowfall can be disastrous as, quite apart from keeping customers at home, the delivery process can become a nightmare. We always hoped for relatively mild nights at peak periods. We were concerned that all the excess stock that we had to store outside in the sheds would be prone to frost damage.

Peak periods? Checklist

✓ Do not underestimate the amount of work peak periods generate.
✓ Keep records of previous years' performances to help you with ordering and organisation.

Giving products away

Every shop will receive a regular stream of requests to donate flowers to all sorts of charitable events. These may be for local schools, clubs, societies, raffles or auctions and it is best to decide at an early stage what your policy is.

I found it very annoying when someone would regularly ask us to donate something, especially if they never bought anything from the shop and you knew that they bought their flowers elsewhere. Consequently we decided we would donate things only to people or organisations who were also customers of the shop.

One of our account customers was the BBC and every year they would ask us to donate something for their charity auction. We were always pleased to deliver a large basket arrangement to them. The fact that they would describe it on the radio, and publicise our name when they auctioned it, was an added bonus. Other local businesses who were good account customers would also ask for bouquets or arrangements. They would either offer them as a raffle prize or auction them at a charitable event and we were only too happy to supply these.

We would politely tell non-customers asking for freebies why we were declining their request. We explained that we received so many similar requests that we had to find a way of keeping our give-aways at a manageable level and thus we only gave them to regular customers. I found that almost everyone felt this was fair and reasonable. As for those who didn't, we felt no obligation to give them anything anyway.

5 Operating expenses

This chapter looks at:

- Rent and leases
- Business rates and refuse disposal
- Water rates
- Heat and light
- Telecommunications
- Insurance
- Finance charges
- Delivery vehicles
- Maintenance and repairs
- Information technology
- Avoiding scams

Most of the different elements of a shop's operating expenses, such as rent, rates and wages, are unavoidable. However, some of them, such as advertising, are optional. For many of these expenses you have a choice of supplier. For some of them you have a choice of whether or not to use a particular service at all.

Every shop will be pestered almost daily by people trying to convince you that they have a service or a product that is exactly right for your needs. It will be far better than whatever similar service or product you might be using now. These calls can be very annoying, especially on a busy day.

It is a good idea to develop techniques for quickly identifying time wasters and cutting them short. Some cold callers will not be put off by a polite refusal. Sometimes you have to be extremely blunt and firm to stop them wasting your time. As well as being annoying, the caller may well be tying up a phone line that a customer is trying to use to place an order.

Rent and leases

Having negotiated the rent at the beginning of a lease or upon taking over a shop there is little you can do to change it until either the next rent review is due or the current lease needs renewing. At the time of taking out a new lease you should know just what you are committing yourself to.

Most leases require the lessee to take responsibility for maintaining the property in good condition and for any repairs or renewals.

> When we acquired the Cambridge shop we were taking a lease on an old property that was not in the best condition.
>
> We were concerned that at the end of the lease the landlord might claim we were leaving the property in a worse condition than we found it. We did not want to be liable for costly repairs and redecoration. Consequently we hired a local surveyor to produce a 'schedule of condition'. This consisted of a file detailing the condition of all aspects of the property, together with photographs to back it up.
>
> This exercise cost us about £600 and was not an essential expense at the time. However, it did provide us with peace of mind. The motivation for doing this is the same as the choice of whether or not to have a full survey done when you are buying a house.

It is also common practice for a lease to contain a clause stating when the rent will next be reviewed and this also needs negotiating. You will want this review to be as far into the duration of the lease as possible. Often the wording of the lease suggests that rent reviews will only ever be upwards, and this too is worthy of negotiation. The local area might fall into decline, or rents generally take a tumble because of an economic recession. If so, you would have good grounds to negotiate a decrease in rent at the time of a review.

If your landlord asks for an unreasonable rent increase you should employ a surveyor who will assess market rates for similar shops in your area and negotiate accordingly. Before doing this, however, it is worth examining how the surveyor will be paid for his work. It is quite common for the surveyor's fee to be a percentage of the final rent negotiated. This is bizarre because it means that the worse the job the surveyor does the higher your bill will be! When I employed a surveyor we agreed upon a completely different method. I worked out a scale of charges that rewarded him for driving the agreed rent down to the lowest level he could possibly achieve.

The Royal Institute of Chartered Surveyors offers a special scheme for 'Rent Reviews for Small Businesses'. This includes a fixed scale of reasonable charges.

Rent and leases? Checklist

✓ Time spent reading a lease fully and carefully is never wasted.

✓ Consult a legal adviser if necessary. Your local Business Link will provide free general advice and information about the Lawyers for Business scheme.

Business rates and refuse disposal

Business rates are levied by your local authority and relate to the size and location of the premises. It is well worth checking that the square footage figures they are working to are correct. It is also a good idea to chat to neighbouring shop proprietors to compare notes. If you feel you are paying too much you can appeal.

There are many people who offer a service to get your rates reduced for you. These services usually operate on a 'no win – no fee' basis and an experienced firm using qualified surveyors can win you significant savings. I would suggest taking time to check them out very carefully, however. The small print of any agreement you enter into should be studied closely. There are many dubious characters operating in this field.

It is normal practice these days to be charged separately by your local authority for refuse collection. The scale of charges will relate to the number and size of your bins. Make sure that you have the correct capacity for your business. I found that the best approach was to pay for whatever bin capacity you would need for a typical week's business.

We found that it definitely helped to be on good terms with the bin men. There were some busy days when we simply forgot to put the bins outside. They would always come into the shop to remind us and collect our bins. When there was just a small amount of overflow rubbish they wouldn't complain. And at peak times such as Christmas, Valentine's Day and Mother's Day, when we had lots of overspill rubbish, that relationship paid off. Taking your own rubbish to the local tip can be very expensive. The one and only time I did this I was charged £30. Giving our bin men an occasional £5 tip was much more cost-effective. In some areas there are alternative services to those provided by, or through, your local authority and so it may be worth shopping around.

Water rates

The main thing to check here is whether it is most cost-effective to pay a fixed scale charge or to have your supply metered, assuming that you have a choice.

> Our Cambridge shop occupied space that had originally been three adjoining terraced houses. There were two different points for the water supply. Consequently we received two quite separate invoices for water and sewerage. One of these supply points serviced the workroom. We used considerable volumes of water here so we were happy to pay the fixed scale charges for this. The other serviced a part of the shop where there was a tap and a second lavatory. As this area was only lightly used we had it metered.
>
> When we had been at the Cambridge shop for a couple of years the Water Board undertook some major work to renew the water main in a nearby road. This necessitated the closure of that road for several weeks and the closure of one lane of the road outside our shop. I took the view that this was disruptive to our business and was causing a significant loss of passing trade. A claims assessor worked on behalf of us and neighbouring shopkeepers to seek compensation from the Water Board.
>
> To enable the assessor to submit a strong case I had to provide a lot of detailed accounting information. They needed me to demonstrate how much our sales had suffered. However, it was all worth it when we finally received a substantial cheque. All of the assessor's costs were met by the Water Board.

Heat and light

Now that most people have so many choices of supplier for electricity, gas and oil it is well worth shopping around. There is a limit to how much time you should spend on this, however. If you were to listen to every potential supplier who visited the shop, or called on the phone, you would waste far more time and money than you might save.

The potential savings can be presented in very misleading ways. If you do seriously consider changing supplier be sure to study the small print carefully first. There are independent web sites that compare the different charges made by different suppliers and these are well worth a look.

Whoever your supplier is there are usually good savings to be made if you pay by direct debit. This now applies to many essential services.

I once switched supplier having checked the small print in great detail only to find that the administration relating to the change was horrendous. I wasted a lot of time and emotion on phone calls and letters in my attempts to have incorrect invoices put right. Eventually I switched back to the original supplier.

The lesson I decided to learn from this was that my current supplier was never going to charge me much more than anyone else. Thus I would save time and money by never changing again. I would spend no time listening to any alternative suppliers. I may have spent a little more but sometimes you just have to put a real value on your own time.

It is of course always wise to read your own meter occasionally and check it against your invoices. Our shop also contained the electric meters for some flats above the shop. The meter readers were often confused by this and made many mistakes.

Telecommunications

For many shops telecommunications can represent a large part of their total operating expenses. As with other utilities there are now all sorts of options other than BT. Again it is well worth studying the small print of the charging methods used by the different providers. What may seem like wonderful savings when the salesperson is talking to you can seem hard to detect when the bills come in. I chopped and changed different suppliers and services over the years. I still found that when adding up my total telecom costs for a complete year there were never any big savings.

I found that I would have spent much the same over the years if I had continued using BT for everything. However, be careful even if you do opt for a quiet life and stick with BT. Their range of services is now so complex and diverse that they need studying periodically to ensure you are still getting a good deal.

I have always found that minimising the number of lines in a shop can be a false economy. Some shops that have just one line for customers to use to place an order will lose a lot of orders when that line is engaged. It is obvious that many customers have either Yellow Pages or a similar directory in front of them when they place an order. If they get an engaged tone they simply move straight onto the next florist.

A large shop will need multiple lines not just for inbound customer calls but also for other purposes. You may need a dedicated line for things like the credit card machine, the relay service computer, a relay service freephone number, fax machine, etc. We also had a separate number that was reserved for calls from our suppliers and for our own outgoing calls.

For all the lines from which we made outgoing calls, we used a service from a third party that greatly reduced the cost per call. We also paid for calls to be diverted to us from numbers that had been previously been used by nearby florist shops that had since closed down. Every quarter I would study these bills to track how many calls had been diverted to us to ensure that these services were still cost-effective.

If you use a computerised relay system then you may want to opt for a broadband link. This provides you with a dedicated line, providing both high-speed data transmission and speech calls.

> If your telecom services are disrupted through no fault of your own then you should record all the details and seek compensation. One day we found that some of our phone lines were dead. I then noticed a man at the top of the telegraph pole across the road. Upon questioning him I found that he was a contractor working on behalf of one of the major telecom companies. It was planned work that we should have been notified of weeks before. I submitted a claim for compensation and this was duly settled in full.
>
> On another occasion BT made a mistake in implementing a new call divert service for us. They cut off two of our main lines for more than a day. Again I claimed for compensation for loss of business and they paid up in full very quickly.

Insurance

It is also worth shopping around for the best deals for shop, buildings and van insurance. This does not always mean that cheapest is best. The amounts covered on the general shop insurance should certainly be checked carefully. The companies that advertise in the *Florist & Wholesale Buyer* are worth checking out. They have identified florist shops as a specialist vertical market and have tailored their insurance packages accordingly.

Vehicle insurance for the vans can vary greatly depending upon the provider and the drivers for whom you need cover. Drivers under the age of 25 can prove very expensive, as can anyone who does not have a clean licence. Some insurers will place a limit on the number of drivers covered. Most will charge an administration fee for any changes you might need to make as the staff change. A policy that guarantees you a replacement vehicle in the event of problems is well worth paying a little extra for.

Some time spent surfing the Internet can also find some worthwhile savings if you deal directly with an insurance company without going through a broker.

Finance charges

Most banks will offer free banking services for perhaps the first eighteen months. After that bank charges can prove costly, so again you need to study the small print before opening a new account. Once you get past the free banking period the charges can be quite a shock. Examine the monthly statements to see how you can keep these charges to a minimum. Using the bank's online banking system will usually help you save money. Once I saw what our bank was charging us for paying in cash I stopped doing this. Instead of taking cash to the bank I used our cash takings to pay our suppliers.

Ironically our bank implemented some hefty increases in their charges for business accounts at about the same time that they cancelled their regular weekly order for flowers. They told me they were very sorry but they just could not afford fresh flowers any more!

Online banking can make it much easier to shuffle your money between accounts to maximise your interest. We had current accounts for the shop and our personal money and also an online high interest account. Each night I looked at what was in each account and thought about any immediate outgoings. I then switched money between accounts to keep just enough in the shop current account and as much as possible in the high interest account.

Changing banks can be a real headache. Even though most of them offer to handle most of the work involved in changing direct debits and standing orders there are plenty of other problems that occur.

Most shops send invoices to their account customers and receive payments straight into their accounts via the BACS system. It can involve a lot of work and hassle getting all your account customers to change your banking details on their online banking system.

There is a range of different suppliers for the credit and debit card processing services you will need and their rates can vary significantly. In our first little shop we were paying a service charge of over 3 per cent on credit card transactions. When we took over a larger shop we found that Interflora had negotiated a great deal with one particular service and we were able to reduce charges to only a fraction over 1 per cent. The rates do of course depend upon the volume of card transactions. We found that as our card sales rose to some £200,000 per year the savings became very significant.

Delivery vehicles

When buying a new delivery vehicle it is very nice if you have the cash to fund an outright purchase. It is very difficult to get a better deal than a well-negotiated cash purchase. Some people will argue that you might be better off entering into a leasing arrangement for a van and invest your cash in some other aspect of the business but I have never found this made sense.

Instead of a traditional van it can be very tempting to acquire some sort of MPV (multi-purpose vehicle). This could be used mostly for deliveries with the seats down but also for ferrying the children around with the seats up. The problem with this is that you cannot reclaim the VAT on the purchase. You can only do this for a proper van with no side windows behind the driver's cab.

If you do not have the cash available for outright purchase then there are very good tax efficient leasing deals available. Again you should shop around and study the small print carefully.

I have always found that if you do all the sums over the lifetime of a van, diesel engines are usually more cost effective than petrol. There are now diesel vans that will return some 50 miles per gallon around town and will usually prove reliable for the best part of 150,000 miles. The purchase price will be higher but the savings on fuel will usually outweigh this.

Paying for your fuel can be very easily managed with a fuel card for each driver. This way the drivers never need cash from the till for fuel. You receive a monthly VAT invoice that is best paid by direct debit. Again it is worth shopping around and comparing what you pay per litre on a fuel card against the local pump prices.

Maintenance and repairs

If you are the practical type and can handle most problems and repairs yourself then all well and good. It is as well that all your staff know just who they should contact in the event of a problem.

> Once Liz and I were on holiday in the West Indies when somebody decided to drive around Cambridge on a Saturday night shooting at shop windows. As a result we needed new glass in the main shop window and the front door. This involved much hassle and many phone calls. We had to give Jo, the shop manager, and our son the information they needed to check insurance policies and take appropriate action. This taught me to leave all the insurance details easily accessible in the shop.

As the Cambridge shop was an elderly property with very suspect plumbing I found it was best always to use the same plumber for any problems. He knew where the stopcocks were and could quickly identify weak points in the pipework.

There were only two regular maintenance contracts that we entered into. One was for the refrigeration equipment in the cold room and the other was for the annual checking and maintenance of the fire extinguishers. This was to ensure that we complied with health and safety regulations.

Information technology

Just about every shop will have at least one computer these days. There are excellent software packages available for handling your own accounts and payroll. So long as you are happy that you can get to grips with these they can save you a lot of money. In comparison with using an accountant you could save thousands of pounds if you know what you are doing.

Accounting packages can be bought outright for a modest amount. For an outlay of some £100 per year a contract for payroll software will ensure that your system is kept fully up to date. Every change to taxation rates and codes and any updates to National Insurance rates are all provided on a CD. This subject is covered in more detail in chapter 7, Doing the books.

Many customers now find a florist via the Internet and so a good website is becoming essential for most shops. There are many providers of website services and they differ greatly in the rates they charge and the quality of the service they offer. Some are very inexperienced, operating from their bedroom. Some are very experienced, with in-depth knowledge of computing, telecoms and graphic design.

It is best to seek a website provider through personal recommendation. Examine some of the websites they are responsible for and compare their rates with others. This subject is covered in more detail in chapter 6, Sales and marketing.

When buying consumables it is wise to shop around but I have found that often it pays to avoid the cheapest options. A good example is the sourcing of ink-jet cartridges for printers. Having compared the cost of cartridges from a mainstream supplier such as Hewlett Packard with the many cheaper alternatives, it can seem very easy to save money. However, I have experienced all sorts of problems with cheap alternatives. One mail order supplier frequently sent me the wrong cartridges. In attempting to put things right they just made things worse and I ended up with a sheaf of incorrect invoices and credit notes. Some refilled cartridges proved to be damaged and some were only half filled. Eventually I decided to stop messing around and reverted to buying new HP cartridges. I found they always worked perfectly and lasted so much longer. I may have paid a little more but I no longer wasted time on this task.

Information technology? Checklist

✓ Take advantage of the excellent software packages for accounts and payroll.
✓ A good website is essential.
✓ Choose an experienced web designer.
✓ Shop around for consumables but don't always go for the cheapest option.

Avoiding scams

The level of attempted scams and con tricks is a major annoyance these days. They can waste an awful lot of time for proprietors and their staff.

Often the phone would ring and a voice state that back in February they called you regarding advertising. Although you were too busy at the time, you did promise that you would proceed later in the year. Then they will tell you that the advertising will be placed in a directory/diary/calendar. It is aimed at benefiting the disabled/orphaned children/members of the emergency services/drug awareness, etc. Usually the truth is that you have never made them any promises. The only person who would benefit is the person on the other end of the phone.

Another common call is the one where the caller knows of someone who is about to register your shop name as an Internet domain name. This would enable them to steal lots of business from you. However, if you make an immediate payment to the caller they will get in first and register the name on your behalf. This is *always* a con.

There are several businesses that pretend to be the official Data Protection Registrar. They send you notification that you will be liable for prosecution unless you register with them immediately and send a cheque for over £100. The reality is that, if you do need to register, it costs £35 with the legitimate authority. Many of these businesses are not actually illegal as they will obtain the official registration. They pay the standard fee for you and then claim that they have provided a service to which they are entitled to payment. In fact you can do this just as easily yourself and save a lot of money.

Similar letters from businesses purporting to offer products and services relating to health and safety may also imply that you have to spend money with them. They will say that whatever they are selling is mandatory to comply with current legislation. Many of these are a con and you should seek advice from the official authority if you are unsure.

Credit card cons are a constant problem and will continue to be so even with the advent of chip and PIN machines. These machines greatly improve card security when the customer is in the shop. The biggest problem for florists, however, is with orders placed over the phone. If the 'customer' is using someone else's card you usually will not know there is a problem until the dreaded charge-back letter arrives from the card company. A visit to the recipient of the order will usually elicit the response that they have no idea who the sender is. Usually there will either be no name or a false name on the message card.

Sometimes you can spot a dubious telephone order because it will be for an unusually high value. The caller will often want add-ons such as champagne and chocolates. Some callers are daft enough not to withhold their number and so dialling 1471 is always worth trying after a suspicious call.

> We had one caller who worked for a large department store and decided to send his mother a £50 bouquet on Mother's Day. He paid for it using one of their customer's card details. We worked very closely with the cardholder on this scam as we were determined to nail the offender. Between us we were eventually successful in having him prosecuted. He was fired by his employer and also suffered the shame of his parents finding out exactly what he had done.

Any calls purporting to be from a bank or card company requesting any sort of financial details will almost certainly be bogus. A girl working in one florist shop took a call from someone claiming to be the supplier of the shop's card services. They claimed that they had experienced a major computer system failure. This had resulted in all the card transactions that day having been lost. However, if the shop gave them all the card details over the phone they could enter them manually, so that they would still get paid. If you ever get a call like this put the phone down. Try dialling 1471 in the unlikely event that the caller has not remembered to withhold their number. Then call your card services provider and report what has happened.

I found that contacting the police in the event of credit card fraud is largely a waste of time. No matter how much evidence you might be able to give them, they seem to treat it as low priority and cite low staffing, etc. for their inability to take action. It is also disappointing that the card companies often seem disinclined to take much interest. They seem to take the view that it is such a massive problem that they do not have the manpower to spend much time on each case. They would prefer you to simply accept a charge-back and put it down to experience.

6 Sales and marketing

This chapter looks at:

- Advertising
- Gold cards
- Direct marketing
- Telesales
- Distance selling regulations
- Sales in the shop
- Keeping tabs on your competitors
- Shop hours
- Customer confidentiality

- Looking after your best customers
- Deals with funeral directors
- Networking
- Weddings
- The Internet
- Signage
- Shop layout
- What to do when competitors close down

Although these two aspects of business are frequently linked there is an important difference in emphasis between them. One of the best definitions I have heard is that marketing creates an environment in which selling can take place. Selling is creating the environment in which buying can take place.

To a florist this means that marketing is done through advertising in directories, websites, mailshots, local newspapers and magazines and via your relay service provider. Selling is mostly achieved when a customer walks into the shop or contacts the shop by phone, fax or the Internet.

Advertising

Soon after Liz acquired her first shop we both spent a weekend in Birmingham attending the Spring Florist Event for the first time. We were both very inexperienced and were keen not just to visit all the stands but to talk to lots of people from whom we felt we could learn. We always found this an excellent trade show for just about everyone involved in floristry. Associated workshops are run, focusing on different aspects of the trade. While Liz attended all the design demonstrations I attended the more general business sessions.

One of these sessions addressed sales and marketing and included an open forum. As someone who was at that time entrenched in the computer business, and completely new to floristry, I was very keen to know how we could best spend our little marketing budget. Finding myself in a room full of experienced shop owners I asked them what they felt were the most effective means of marketing their shops. The response I received was absolutely unanimous and it was a response that we remembered from that day onwards: a Yellow Pages advert was a must. A Thomson's Directory advert was probably worthwhile but I would be wasting my money if I spent money on any other form of advertising. The Internet was relatively new in those days but already some people could see the benefits of tapping into this in the future.

For several years we followed this advice pretty much to the letter. We did try a little advertising in the local press but it was indeed a complete waste of money.

We had some flyers and discount cards printed at very low cost by a friend of mine who had a printing business. We hand delivered 5,000 of these through local letterboxes. These cards gave the holder a 10 per cent discount and they were quite effective, with some customers continuing to use them for several years. However, if we had had to pay the true cost of printing, this exercise would not have proved cost-effective.

Over the years I think the pattern has changed in terms of what advertising works and what does not. My current view is that Yellow Pages is still well worthwhile but has become very expensive. I also find it annoying that they seem happy to accept advertising from anyone who will pay for it. This has led to entries from many dubious operators, who are not florist shops but want to give the impression they are, appearing among genuine listings. Many florists are now questioning the very high advertising costs of directory advertising. The new classified directory section in the front of BT's Phone Book is increasingly effective. Many customers are becoming used to having just one directory next to their telephone. This is likely to hurt both Yellow Pages and Thomson's Directory in the future.

We always received many approaches from all sorts of local newspapers and magazines wanting us to take advertising space. We were polite and friendly but always declined their many special offers. When I talk to other shopkeepers who have spent money on local advertising I invariably find they regret it.

It may be appealing to place an advertisement in a glossy local magazine. Often these magazines will offer to produce an 'advertorial' to accompany your advert. This will be very flattering and it may seem like excellent PR but I think these are very difficult to justify in terms of cost. Calculating how many extra orders you would need to make enough additional profit to cover the costs should bring you back down to earth. The sales person at the magazine will tell you all about the less quantifiable benefits of visibility and awareness. My advice is to be dubious and cautious.

Advertising? Checklist

✓ Calculate your budget for advertising carefully.
✓ Take out space in your area Yellow Pages and BT classified directory.
✓ Be cautious about other forms of local advertising.

Gold cards

A couple of years ago Interflora introduced a new Gold Card initiative for its members. These are credit card size and carry the shop name, address and phone number and the Interflora logo. One of these cards is attached to every order before it is handed to the recipient. I found these very effective as most people retained them and put them in their wallet or handbag. We frequently saw them when a customer in the shop opened their wallet or purse to pay for flowers.

These cards cost some £70 per thousand and I am sure they provide an excellent return on the investment. When delivering flowers I made sure the gold card was prominently displayed on the product. I believe it added to the recipient's impression that they were receiving a high-quality gift.

Direct marketing

This is certainly an area that can bear fruit but making it work is very hard work. Soon after taking over the Cambridge shop we found that despite being the nearest florist to all the businesses on the Cambridge Science

Park, the shop had never done a mail shot there. I sent a letter extolling the virtues of brightening up their reception areas with fresh flowers to the Receptionist of each company. I then followed this up by telephone.

This met with only limited success although some of the companies did become regular account customers. Some would want fresh flowers supplied and delivered each Monday morning – this was great but it did mean that the already busy Monday mornings became even more hectic.

We decided to try a more direct approach with each new business that moved into the area. We would take them a modern arrangement for their reception area as a welcome gift. We used the opportunity to tell them all about the services we provided and explained that the arrangement was simply a gift from us and they were under no obligation to spend any money. We found this worked very well and most of these businesses decided to use us for something. They would place *ad hoc* orders, even if they did not want flowers every week. Every company that we gave a freebie to subsequently used us for something.

Cold calling is very hard work and we found that no matter what approach we took it was an unpleasant task. We preferred to expend time and effort on other things. It obviously works for a lot of people because so much time and money is invested in cold calling, but it never worked for us.

> When I was in the IT industry I visited a number of the best known and most successful specialist telemarketing/telesales businesses. I was amazed at how often their carefully scripted calls were met with very aggressive and obscene responses. Most of their operators became hardened to the job over time. Yet I still saw some of them reduced to tears by the abuse they received. I once sat next to a girl who was cold calling people to try to interest them in an upgrade to their computer system. I was staggered when I overheard three of the first five people she called telling her to '**** off'.
>
> We decided we did not want to become known as that really annoying florist who cold calls people like a double glazing company.

Telesales

For most florists telesales mean receiving inbound calls from a customer. This is very different from outbound calls, where you are hoping there is a slight chance that the person you are calling may be interested in what you have to offer.

Inbound calls typically come from people who have already decided to buy and are calling you to place an order. We found that 90 per cent of inbound calls resulted in an order. Those who did not order were often people who thought they could have a bouquet delivered for £15 or less and could not imagine spending more than that on flowers.

The impact you make when receiving an inbound call depends on just how you handle it. You have the opportunity to influence the customer in deciding what to order and how much to spend.

When we took over the Cambridge shop we were appalled to hear the girls answer the phone and then say the dreaded words 'Bouquets start at £20'. This almost always resulted in the customer placing an order for £20 plus delivery. By learning how to develop a sale over the phone the girls quickly saw how easy it could be to increase the size of the bouquet to £30 or more. They could also offer chocolates, a balloon and maybe even a teddy bear and champagne.

Interflora were very helpful in providing their preferred sales script to all their member shops and our telephone sales technique was frequently tested by them. They would call pretending to be a customer and record the call. We would then receive a copy of the recording on a tape or CD, together with an assessment report.

I believe that the ideal script is slightly different from the Interflora recommendation. I learned from big professional telesales businesses that the sequence of the call structure is absolutely essential.

An example of my favoured script is as follows.

1 *Good morning, Biggs Florist, how can I help you?*
Do not say the shop name first as many callers do not take in the first one or two words of your response.

2 *Can I take a contact telephone number for you please, Mr Smith?*
Customers are more inclined to proceed with an order if they know you already have a means of contacting them. As a form of address you should usually use whatever means of address the customers themselves use. If the customer identifies himself as John Smith then call him John and if he uses Mr Smith do the same. This can vary with some customers, however, and you have to use your discretion. You can probably tell from 'Mary Smith's' voice whether or not she is likely to prefer to be called Mrs Smith.

3 *When would you like this delivered?*
Check both the day and the date.

4 *Can I please take the name and address of the recipient, Mr Smith?*
Again, taking address details at an early stage increases the likelihood that the caller will proceed with an order.

5 *What would you like to order?*

6 *Bouquets range in price from £20 for the smallest to £95 and over for the largest and most luxurious. May I ask what the occasion is?*

7 *For a silver wedding anniversary people usually spend at least £50 on the bouquet to get something really special.*

8 *We do also sell very nice helium balloons with a 'Congratulations on your Silver Wedding' message. This could be attached to the bouquet and would cost an extra £4.*

9 *We also sell other extras like champagne and chocolates for very special occasions.*

10 *What message would you like to go on a card to be attached to the flowers?*

11 *So that will be a total of £89.95 to cover the bouquet, a balloon, chocolates and delivery.*
Do not mention the delivery charge until you reach this stage and state it in a matter of fact way, as it is a standard part of the order. Never say it in an apologetic way or suggest that it may be open to negotiation.

12 *How would you like to pay? We accept all major credit and debit cards.*
Take the card type, number, expiry date and the last three digits of the number on the signature strip on the back of the card.

13 *May I please take the address that your card statements are sent to. This is probably your home address.*

14 *Thank you for your order, Mr Smith. The amount of £89.95 will be debited from your account within three working days. I will ensure that we deliver your order on Wednesday 15th March.*
All the details of delivery date, names, addresses, card message and debit/credit card details should be very carefully repeated.

Never assume that the caller is poor and always state the full range of prices. I often answered the phone and tried to assess the caller. I might guess that she was an old lady struggling on her pension and then find that she was quite happy to spend well over the minimum. Conversely we had extremely posh, titled customers who thought £20 was a fortune.

Philip Coy is an Interflora director who built up a very large and successful telesales operation and was always willing to pass on hints and tips to Interflora members. I remember him telling me that the least successful telesales operators he had ever employed were florists. They always seemed to assume that the caller would have very little money to spend. He discovered that people from completely different backgrounds were usually more successful in talking up the value of each sale.

We introduced an incentive scheme for our staff that related to the average value of all the orders we received. Before long people who had previously been selling lots of £20 gift-wrapped bouquets were boasting about the size of the order each time they put the phone down. There would be much good-natured banter as the details of big sales were broadcast around the workroom. There was much mickey taking when somebody took a small order with no add-ons.

It is still vitally important to be just as courteous when the customer wants to spend only a small amount. It is possible to leave the customer feeling good about the way you handled their order, regardless of how much they spend. The main thing is to let the customer know what the options are and then they can make up their own mind. Somebody who places a small order today may place bigger orders in the future.

It has been suggested to me that if some people can only afford to spend the minimum then it is wrong to talk about bouquets that cost far more. I totally disagree with this viewpoint. I believe that customers deserve to be told about the full range of options available to them.

Telesales? Checklist

✓ Remember that first impressions over the phone are as important as first impressions in the shop.
✓ Invest time in staff training in telephone sales techniques.

Distance selling regulations

Anyone selling goods or services via the Internet, by mail order, or by phone or fax, should be aware of the Consumer Protection Regulations 2000. The key features of these regulations are as follows:

- clear information about the goods or services offered must be provided for the consumer;
- the consumer must be sent confirmation after making a purchase;
- the consumer is entitled to a cooling-off period of seven working days, where appropriate.

Clear and comprehensible information must be made available to the consumer to enable them to decide whether or not to buy. This information includes:

- the seller's name and postal address;
- a description of the goods or services;
- the total price, including taxes;
- delivery costs where applicable;
- arrangements and date for delivery;
- the right to cancel the order;
- the period for which the price remains valid.

When an order has been placed the seller must send the consumer a confirmation by post, fax or email.

Sales in the shop

When the customer is actually present in the shop the sales approach should be similar to the telephone example above. However, shop sales can be personalised much more.

This was an area where Liz really excelled. I have watched a customer walk into the shop to be greeted by Liz with a big smile and ask how she could help. The man stated that he wanted 'a bunch of flowers for about a tenner'. Liz chatted to him and found out about the occasion, his girlfriend's likes and dislikes and made some small talk. He eventually walked out with a £30 hand-tied bouquet with a balloon, teddy and chocolates attached and with a big smile on his face. He also had one of our Gold Cards and Liz's business card in his wallet.

Liz made flower buying a real pleasure for people and many of the people who met her became regular customers. We all learned from her technique. The biggest factor in our growth came not so much from an increased volume of orders but from greatly increased order values. The girls became very adept at getting to know the regular customers, using their name and engaging them in friendly banter. If customers had to wait for something special to be made, they could sit on a sofa and we would offer them tea or coffee and a magazine or newspaper to read.

It is so important to greet any customer entering the shop. Even if the only member of staff present is halfway through making a hand tied bouquet they can still say 'Hello' and smile welcomingly. The customer will almost invariably be understanding. In fact we often found the customer was interested in watching the make-up work while they waited and would request something similar.

Even if someone entering the shop is only seeking directions it pays to be pleasant and helpful. If you go out of your way to help they will remember this and may well become a customer in the future. Once a lady was taken ill outside our shop. We helped her inside, sat her down and made her a cup of tea while we phoned her husband. We only did what most people would have done but they became good customers from that day on.

One very useful thing we did was to file all the old orders in the office area at the rear of the shop as we found that we often had to refer back to them. A customer might contact us to say that he wanted an anniversary bouquet for his wife. He wanted an exact repeat of what we had delivered the year before as his wife loved it, but he could not describe what it was. We would be able to trace the order from the previous year and find out what we had produced and what the flower content was.

Some shops now maintain a customer database that includes details of special occasions like birthdays and anniversaries. The computer might notify you that Mr Smith's wedding anniversary is coming up next week. If he has not ordered anything for this, a friendly phone call to remind him can win a good order. If he says that he is taking Mrs Smith away somewhere for the anniversary and will not be ordering flowers, no problem. You can then say that the main thing is that he had not forgotten and you didn't want him to get into trouble! You could take the opportunity to offer to arrange for flowers to be placed in their hotel room. Many people love this sort of special service and are happy to pay for it. It makes them feel that you are acknowledging them as a good customer and giving them special treatment.

Frequently customers have no idea what they want and a good sales person will find out what the occasion is and develop the sale accordingly. Many men feel nervous walking into a florist shop. They do not know anything about flowers. They do not know their wife or girlfriend's favourite flowers or colours. They may feel embarrassed if they are asked questions they cannot answer. It is better for the sales person to lead the conversation and make appropriate suggestions. These sales are very good opportunities for the florist. They can be high value orders tailored to what is in stock at the time.

Different people have very different tastes. If a customer insisted on a strange mix of flowers wrapped up in what the girls referred to as 'prostitute pink' cellophane, then that is what they got, even if the florists had a quiet laugh in the workroom afterwards.

> Liz had one customer who wanted one dead flower delivered to his girlfriend's office at 10am. This was to be followed by ten dozen red roses delivered at 11am. Liz made very sure that when the first delivery was made there was nothing with the shop name accompanying it!

When the customer is present the easiest way to make a good sale is often to show them examples of high value orders that have just been made. Frequently people will simply say 'That looks great, I'll have one of those, please'. Then the opportunity exists to show them how add-ons can enhance their order even further.

I have never seen the need for having a big sale in a florist shop. In my experience the vast majority of people who visited our shop actually bought something. If we had implemented some sort of grand sale I suspect it would have attracted very few extra customers. It would often have reduced the takings for something that the customer would have been prepared to pay the full price for. However, there is a point in marking down slow moving plants and giftware, etc.

All staff should, of course, be smart and consistent in their appearance. A uniform appearance can be achieved very simply by giving everyone a clean tabard to wear. This should clearly display the shop name and preferably also the relay service the shop belongs to.

Sales in the shop? Checklist

✓ Develop your and your staff's sales techniques.
✓ Make sure the shop and staff have a welcoming appearance.
✓ Remember that people skills can be converted into sales!

Keeping tabs on your competitors

No matter how well your shop is performing you can never ignore what your competitors are doing. Learn what you can from your visiting wholesalers but take what they say with a pinch of salt. Some florists will only tell their wholesalers things that they want to be passed onto other shops. Often wholesalers form their own view of how a particular shop is doing by what the shop is buying and how busy the florists are.

We always found that most wholesalers loved to gossip. If you treated them with respect and made them a cup of tea it was possible to learn all sorts of things.

If your competitors are doing some sort of special promotion or changing their method of advertising you need to know. If they need more or fewer staff you will want to know, as it is an indicator of how well they are doing.

Often wholesalers would moan about how long it was taking for them to get paid by a particular shop. Sometimes they would tell stories about a shop that had owed them thousands of pounds for well over six months. All of this information helps you to assess the competition and to ensure that you are poised to take advantage of any opportunities that may arise if a nearby shop suddenly closes down.

If a competitor changes their delivery charges, or offers a later cut-off time for same day orders, you want to know before a customer tells you. If a competitor starts to promote free delivery you will want to counter this. You can explain to your customers that there is no such thing and that fewer flowers go into each order to cover the cost of so-called free delivery.

It is also good to keep an objective eye on the quality levels of other shops. When delivering to a funeral director I would always have a good look at the items delivered by the other local florists. I found there was a direct correlation between the quality of each shop's products and the general perception of that shop. Shops that had a reputation for being cheap and cheerful did indeed deliver products that reflected this. Shops with a quality image and a good reputation consistently delivered good work and good quality flowers.

Shop hours

The opening hours of a shop will depend upon many different factors. To some extent you need to fit in with other shops in the immediate vicinity.

If your shop is in a town centre or in a parade of shops then customers will expect all the shops to keep similar hours.

> On weekdays we opened from 8.30am to 5pm. In practice we were almost always open at 8am because that was usually when we arrived. There always seemed to be some early deliveries to make and we were keen to get ready for the day ahead. We usually closed late, either because we had late customers or were still tidying up at the end of the day. We took the view that if we were at the shop anyway then we might as well be open.
>
> Ideally we should have stayed open until 6pm to catch all the end of day opportunities as customers were on their way home but we felt our day was long enough as it was. Had we ever fallen on hard times we knew that staying open that extra hour would boost sales.
>
> On a Saturday we closed at 4.30pm. Although we did not get many walk in customers on a Saturday afternoon we usually had appointments booked for wedding consultations. Also we started make-up work on a Saturday afternoon for the weekly office deliveries that had to be made early on the Monday morning.

Florist shops are usually open for business every day of the year except for Sundays and public holidays. The main exception is of course Mother's Day and also Valentine's Day if it falls on either a Sunday or a Monday. At Easter we found that if we opened on Good Friday sales were typically around half those of a normal trading day. Opening on either Easter Sunday or Monday was a complete waste of time and after trying this once or twice we gave up. Sales on the Saturday of Easter weekend were usually up on a normal Saturday.

Many florists will close for the whole of the period between Christmas Day through to New Year's Day but we never did. We found that sales were very good in that week. There are so many people on holiday who are tired of eating, drinking and watching TV. They want to get out of the house and are likely to be in a shopping mood. The only problem is finding a wholesaler prepared to deliver fresh stock in that week.

Customer confidentiality

Discretion is obviously vitally important because of the very personal nature of many orders and accompanying messages. A florist is frequently asked to promise the customer that they will not divulge the sender's name, or any other details, to the recipient.

At Valentine's Day we always received a number of calls from people pleading with us to divulge the sender's details but unless we could get the sender's permission we would not do so. Often when calling the customer in this sort of situation we would find that they had given us a false name or telephone number anyway. The only exception we ever made was to divulge the sender's details to the police if they requested it.

Some recipients will ask you to tell them where the order came from. If it is a relay order they want to know which town it was sent from. You should never divulge even this much information as often it is sufficient for them to know exactly who the sender is.

> We once received a very hostile call from a school headmistress demanding to know why we had delivered red roses to a 14-year-old pupil. It turned out that the flowers were from a 40-year-old man who was stalking her. We had no way of knowing the recipient was a pupil: she could have been a teacher or anyone else working at the school.
>
> At the end of one Valentine's Day, after we had finally locked the doors, a lady repeatedly knocked on the door. She demanded to know whom her flowers were from and said she would not leave until we told her. After we politely refused she produced her warrant card – she was an off duty police-woman. We still would not tell her, and she was very angry, but the sender had been adamant about his anonymity.

It can be quite amusing when people place multiple orders for flowers to go to different people on Valentine's Day. I remember once taking an order in the shop from a small bespectacled man in a three-piece suit. He sent bouquets to six different ladies, all with quite racy messages attached.

You should never knowingly allow a customer to send a message containing obscene words, however. It is a matter of discretion that sometimes you need to suggest some more appropriate wording.

Looking after your best customers

In the run-up to Christmas each year we would get out the previous year's customer lists. This showed whom we had sent either a card or a diary to in the previous year. To our best 100 customers we would send a small gift costing not much more than £3. I always found that a diary was the most acceptable gift. It is practical and likely to be kept in the recipient's handbag or briefcase. It can display your shop name, telephone number and website address. When I considered changing the gift to a calendar or a pen, I first sounded out several of our account customers. They all told me that they had come to rely on getting a diary from us every year and so would be disappointed if we changed to a different gift.

We sent these diaries to regular account customers, other regulars and also to brides whose wedding flowers we had provided in the previous year. I would either mail these or deliver them personally in early October. People in senior positions are given diaries by several different suppliers. By getting in early we had the best chance that they would choose to use our diary in preference to others.

Christmas cards were sent to a wider list of good customers in early December. Early Christmas cards tend to have more impact than those received just before Christmas. Many of these served as very effective reminders to people to order their Christmas flowers in good time.

For a handful of our very best customers (people who spent several thousands of pounds on flowers in a year) I would personally deliver a modern arrangement to them in the week before Christmas. As the marketing people always say, the best customers are the ones you've already got. It is far easier to keep your existing customers happy, and spending money with you, than it is to find new customers.

From time to time it is a good idea to look at your sales ledger records to see which of your account customers have not ordered anything for a while. You can make a courtesy telephone call to them politely asking why they seem to have stopped using you. Enquire if there is any problem that you should know about.

You will often discover that the receptionist has left and the replacement was unaware they had an account set up for flowers. If you discover that a customer has stopped using you because they are unhappy about something, deliver a complimentary item to try to win them back.

Deals with funeral directors

This is an area that we never really focused upon. We found that we received as much funeral business as we wanted directly from customers.

Consequently we saw no need to pay funeral directors for any orders they might take on our behalf. However, I know this works very well for some florists and order volumes from the larger funeral directors can be very lucrative.

Many florists produce marketing literature specifically for a funeral director they have an agreement with. This is usually a book with details, illustrations and prices of all the different floral tributes from which the customer can make a selection. The cost to the customer can be included in the total account for all the funeral services provided. The florist usually receives a monthly payment from the funeral director, less the agreed commission fees.

The commission fee can vary enormously and I know of arrangements where the discount given has ranged from 10 per cent to 25 per cent. A lot of these arrangements are of very long standing. If a particular shop has provided a good reliable service to a funeral director for a number of years and developed a friendly relationship this can be a very difficult account for another shop to capture.

Often a funeral director's preferred florist will only change after instances of poor service or complaints from customers. To bid for one of these accounts will often mean having to offer a larger discount than they currently receive. Then you really do have to look hard at the real net profit you will make on the orders. If you have to give a discount of 20 per cent and provide free delivery, this may leave you with very little return for a lot of hard work.

We liked to deal directly with family and friends who wanted to select and order funeral flowers and we used a private area of the shop for this purpose. We found that people were likely to break down in tears when deciding upon their card message. We learned to give them time and privacy and, if appropriate, the age-old solution of tea and sympathy.

Networking

Networking is something that every florist shop owner will do every day by simply talking to people. However, it can pay to join a more formal networking group to promote your business.

I belonged to the Cambridge branch of BNI (Business Network International), which I found to be very effective. A group of some forty people representing all sorts of small businesses in the local area would meet at the ungodly hour of 6.30am every Tuesday. After a working breakfast we then had a strictly timetabled meeting that lasted from 7am to 8.30am.

Each member had a 60-second slot in which to promote their business and make it as interesting as possible. This meant new ideas, funny stories, songs, poems or anything that grabbed people's attention and made them aware of your business.

The idea was that all the members of the group would positively promote all the other members' products and services. Only one member of each profession was involved in a single chapter of the organisation. As the only florist I worked together with a printer, insurance broker, cake maker, carpet cleaner, website designer, leaflet distributor, courier service, driving instructor, solicitor, estate agent, accountant, sign-writer and many others, to learn about their businesses.

The most important part of the meeting was the referrals section. In the previous week every member was expected to find at least one business opportunity for one of the other members of the group. One week I might pass on the details that one of my staff wanted her carpets cleaning and would be expecting a call from the member who specialised in this area. The next week I would pass on the details of a customer's car insurance renewal. The insurance contact would then attempt to find them a better deal. Continually finding these referrals was hard work but it was what made the whole venture work. Every week I left the meeting with at least one order for flowers and at peak periods I always left with several.

> Following Liz's death I decided to sell my Jaguar car, which had a personalised number plate, and to buy a more sensible and economical car. One member of the group had a business called Vehicle Solutions. He came up with a complete solution that maximised the value of the car I was selling, and the number plate, and also reduced the price I paid for the new car. This proved far better than any deal I was offered by any of the car dealers I approached.

Like so many things in life, what you got out of this network depended on what you put into it. Some people found it incredibly difficult to drag themselves out of bed in time for a 6.30am meeting. As a morning person, who always enjoyed getting to the shop early, this was never a problem for me.

Each week one member would have a ten-minute slot in which to promote their business in more detail. Fortunately my turn came just before Valentine's Day. After explaining all the Valentine's Day specials we were promoting, I gave each member a red rose. I also gave the winner of the weekly raffle an impressive hand-tied bouquet. I left that meeting with lots of orders.

There are various similar networking organisations, including the Chamber of Commerce, and I would recommend that you check what exists in your local area.

Apart from the many orders we received through BNI we got lots of good PR. I loved all the occasions when another member would stand up and tell the whole meeting that our shop had provided flowers for their wife/mother/whoever and that they were absolutely fantastic.

The annual membership fee for BNI was £350 but I found it was hard to get better value than this from my marketing budget.

Weddings

Any florist shop is likely to be targeted by anyone putting on a wedding fair. These events are usually held in a local hotel where the suppliers of wedding services can promote their services to couples planning their wedding.

Wedding fairs can be quite expensive because, in addition to the fee charged by the organisers, you will incur a variety of further costs. You have to provide the flowers, accessories and the labour used to make up whatever you choose to put on show. Then you have to provide labour to man the stand on the day. You will need to win bookings for several weddings to cover the costs of the event and enable you to make a reasonable profit.

The majority of florists consider these fairs a waste of time and money. We considered that we won enough wedding orders through our other marketing efforts and, very importantly, by word of mouth recommendations. We did not need to attend wedding fairs. The average return on the investment required is very small. If you are lucky enough to win several really big orders then it can pay off, but this is unlikely.

What we did find very effective was a link with the Cambridge branch of Debenhams, who did attend many of the local wedding fairs. In return for our supplying sample wedding arrangements for them to display within the store and at wedding fairs, they promoted our wedding services. They also supplied us with mannequins and wedding dresses that we used in our window display. This was a good arrangement with both parties promoting the services of the other.

As with funeral arrangements, we designated one area of the shop for customers to sit down with a florist and look at our albums of wedding flower photographs. There was also an album containing the many thank you letters we received from brides and grooms and their parents. This area also had display examples of brides' bouquets, etc., made up with artificial flowers, and many wedding books and magazines for stimulating ideas.

Following the wedding consultation we would provide a detailed price quotation. If the customer then wanted to make a firm booking we requested a £50 non-returnable deposit and the full balance was due two weeks prior to the date of the wedding.

We had one very strange wedding order that worried and completely baffled us. The bride-to-be made several visits to the shop to discuss her wedding plans and to check every last detail. She paid the full price, in advance, in cash, and we duly ordered the flowers and made everything she had asked for. Then we attempted to deliver everything on her big day.

When we called at the address she had given us, the occupants of the house declared that she did not live there and that they had never heard of her. The phone number she had given us returned an unobtainable tone. She had given us an address for the groom but we found that it simply did not exist. We panicked as we assumed that we had made some terrible mistake and taken her details down incorrectly, then calmed down when we realised that she was sure to phone us asking for her flowers.

But we received no phone call and we never saw or heard from her again. The flowers sat in the cold room for a couple of weeks and we eventually threw them away. This was a mystery we never solved. Whether her whole wedding plan was a strange fantasy we never knew, but it certainly distressed us at the time.

The Internet

I am a great believer in a shop having its own professionally designed website. So many potential customers browse and shop this way now and the trend is increasing. Many people now realise that they can find a supplier for all sorts of products and services on the Internet and get the best prices without having to deal with a middleman. This is having a big impact on people like insurance brokers and travel agents – and also on the flower relay services.

Members of Interflora can have a low cost website consisting of a home page describing their shop and a link straight to the main Interflora site. The problem with this is that every order placed in this way will go through the Interflora system and Interflora are entitled to take a cut from each sale. Many members elect to have their own website without any link to the Interflora site. Although this is more expensive to set up and maintain it does mean they can retain more of the proceeds of each order.

The relay services will usually have strict rules preventing the use of their name as a meta-tag in someone else's website. Meta-tags are key words that a customer may use when searching for a florist. Although we could use meta-tags such as 'flowers' and 'Cambridge' we could not use 'Interflora'.

To be fair to Interflora many people have been caught contravening these rights and trying to capitalise on the Interflora brand name. Interflora are clamping down on this and both individual shops and other relay services have found themselves in trouble over it.

Unless you are gifted at website design yourself, and have plenty of time to work on it, it is worth paying for a professional website designer to work on your site for you. Although I had some thirty years' experience in the computer industry and could have set up my own website I chose not to as I have absolutely no aptitude or flair for design. I preferred to use a professional website designer to set up our site. By luck Liz's brother-in-law had such a business and was an obvious choice. He had already designed and set up many websites for different businesses and other organisations. We knew that he could develop an impressive site for us.

There are many people offering website services these days and most of them are still very inexperienced. Many are just dabbling with the Internet and are often operating from their spare room. It is best to find someone through personal recommendation and find out and check the sites they have created. You need to know that your web service provider is a reputable established business that you can rely on to provide a consistent service for years to come. If you take the cheapest option, you may find that person has moved on to some other venture when you need the site updated.

An experienced website provider will ensure that your site can be found by people using Internet search engines such as Google and Yahoo!. You can also have basic entries free of charge in online directories such as Yell and Thomson's and I would recommend paying the relatively small fee for an enhanced listing. This will be far more prominent, give more detail about your shop and contain a link straight to your own website. When we asked Internet customers how they found us the majority would say 'via Yell', the Internet service provided by Yellow Pages.

Another decision is whether or not to enable people accessing your website to place their order online and pay by credit or debit card. We decided not to do this as we preferred people to contact us direct. They would usually browse through the website and then phone us. We could then personalise and maximise the value of the sale.

The drawback to this is that a potential customer in Australia or America will realise that they cannot call you there and then because of the time difference. Some will simply move on to another site that does facilitate online ordering. Having said that, we used to receive many calls from people all over the world. Usually they would tell us that they were looking at a particular product image on their computer screen and they would like to place an order.

I am sure that online ordering will eventually become essential but it does mean that someone needs to be regularly checking a computer in the shop for any urgent orders. It is not something you can check on your home computer at the end of the day.

Even if you decide against having your own website it may well be worth having your preferred domain name registered. This can be done for a small fee and will prevent anyone else using it either to steal orders or to hold you to ransom if you later decide that you have to get on the Internet bandwagon.

You may well receive phone calls from people saying they can register your name because they know of someone else who is planning to do this. They promise that they can save the day for you if you act right away. The idea is that you pay them a sum of several hundred pounds and they register your shop's name and prevent anyone else stealing business from you. If you already have a site they will claim that it is set up wrongly and is hard to find through the search engines. Of course, they can fix this for you. Usually these are people working through the Yellow Pages, searching for businesses without a website address. They call in the hope people will be taken in by their scam and they can make some easy money.

When I received calls like this I would ask for their website address so that I could check their credentials and see how easy they were to find via a search engine. This is a very quick way to terminate this sort of call.

Signage

When we took over both of our shops they had very poor, old-fashioned signage on the shop itself and the delivery vans. One of our first tasks was to replace these as quickly as possible. Bold, fresh signage over the shop is absolutely essential. Once you have it in place you have to make the effort to keep it clean. As the old saying goes, you never get a second chance to make a first impression.

> The single best marketing investment we ever made was to spend £570 on each of the two vans at the Cambridge shop. For this we had on each side a very striking illustration of a hand-tied bouquet and the shop name, address, phone number, website address and Interflora sign. Most of the population of Cambridge seemed to know about us because the vans made such an impression.
>
> Away from the shop, whenever anyone asked us what we did and we told them we owned Biggs Florist, they would tell us they had seen our vans. Even our Yellow Pages sales rep told me that he thought the vans were probably ten times more effective than anything else we were spending our marketing money on.

Before many people enter a shop they will look at the windows or the shop door to see which credit/debit cards are accepted. It is very important to use the stickers provided by the card companies.

Customers also expect you to display the shop opening hours and to be open when you say you are going to be. You will lose some customers for ever if it isn't, even if you leave a sign saying 'Back in ten minutes'. You might get away with this in a remote location where you are the only florist but it is the kiss of death in a busy town centre.

Shop layout

Layout will largely depend on the space you have but it is a good idea to decide on the sort of image you want to project. If you display absolutely everything and leave little space for customers to walk around, this can project an uninviting, cluttered image. It does not encourage the customer to spend much time browsing.

I am always amazed when shopkeepers, with limited available space, display lots of identical items. It is far better to display just one or two examples of each item and give customers more space. Advertisers always talk about the effective use of white space in an advert and I think the same applies in a shop.

Minimalism can be taken too far, of course, as you do not want customers to have the impression that you have a very limited range of stock. If you are not displaying many fresh flowers in the shop because the weather is hot, and most of the stock is in the cold room, then let your customers know. This is an opportunity to impress and inform your customers, who will know that you have facilities to help prolong the life of whatever they might buy. Chilled display cabinets can provide the best of both worlds but they are very expensive and have limited space. If your walk-in trade is big enough then you may be able to justify the cost of them.

As supermarkets demonstrate, the choice of what to display near the point of sale is very important. It makes sense to use this area to display add-ons such as chocolates, teddies, a balloon stand, a greeting card stand and even champagne. Incidentally, you have to be licensed to sell champagne – this involves some form filling, a one-day training course and a court appearance.

Changing the window display regularly can be a chore but we always tried to change ours completely every two weeks. I was surprised at how many people took time to take a good look at the windows, even when the shop was closed. If you fail to do something special for each of the peak periods then people may think you are not making enough of an effort.

Having fresh flowers in the window display is crucial, even though you have to bear the cost of their wastage. Having only artificial flowers on display may save money but does not project the best image. It is worth accepting some stock wastage to tempt in the majority of people who like to see high quality fresh flowers.

Some florists like to display lots of fresh flowers outside the shop. This can look very attractive and is likely to entice more passing trade. Unfortunately this can shorten product life. Flowers do not like traffic fumes and extreme temperatures.

Keeping stock in the shop, or better still in a cold room, will greatly reduce wastage. The ideal situation is probably a compromise. Only put outside stock that you are confident you will sell that day. If your passing trade is not buying outside stock quickly enough, give it to the florists to use for making up orders.

Shop layout? Checklist

✓ Decide on the image you want to project.
✓ Allow your customers enough space to move around.
✓ Think carefully about what to display near the point of sale.
✓ Change the window display reguarly.

What to do when competitors close down

This can be a huge opportunity because even a failing business will have a customer base that will need a new supplier. There will be regular account customers and, most important of all, their phone numbers, which may have been publicised for many years. During our time in Cambridge there were two florist shops that closed down. We managed to get their account customer base and also to have all their telephone calls diverted to us. In each case this resulted in a big surge in our business for very little cost.

Most florist shops will be on good terms with their local competitors as there are many occasions where they can help each other out. We frequently contacted other shops to seek their help when we were in urgent need of something. We might have suddenly needed open lilies for a funeral order, or perhaps a particular size of oasis frame. We were always happy to help other florists out and regularly begged and borrowed from each other. If you decide all your competitors are your enemies, as some florists do, it is unlikely to be in your own best interests.

Some proprietors who are planning to close down will let all their local competitors know and hope to sell their customer base for the highest price they can get. Others will simply close without realising the value of what they possess. If you hear that a competitor is considering closing (and such news often gets around very quickly through the wholesaler grapevine) then act with all possible speed to get in first. This is a not-to-be-missed opportunity: their telephone numbers could win you hundreds of orders. The proprietor may not even ask for financial compensation if you have a good relationship. They may simply want to get out and do something completely different.

For each of the opportunities we had I made sure I was at the shop when they closed their doors for the last time. The proprietor called BT to terminate their phone lines and I then spoke to BT straight away to have all the calls to those numbers diverted to us. It is important to act this quickly as there are telesales businesses around the country that actively look for these sorts of opportunities.

I then contacted their account customers to let them know the shop had closed but that we had reached an agreement with the owner. We would now be looking after them and would provide a similar service. I personally visited account customers who had regularly weekly deliveries, to reassure them that we would continue to provide the services they wanted.

There can, however, be problems related to the type of service that has been provided by a shop that has closed. One small shop that had been our nearest competitor had failed largely because they provided flowers at incredibly low prices. They often included free delivery and could not possibly make a profit.

When their calls were diverted to us we were often asked to deliver the impossible. People would ask for a large bouquet for a total of £15, including free delivery. We would then have to explain that we unable to do this. Most customers would listen to the reasons, accept them and place an order anyway. A small minority would not listen and would accuse us of charging extortionate prices. Those were customers we decided we could not afford to placate.

Conversely another shop that closed was located in a very affluent part of Cambridge. We found that most of their customers were used to spending significantly more than average. The order volumes were not huge but the order values were excellent.

7 Doing the books

This chapter looks at:

- The benefits of DIY accounting
- Drawing up budgets and targets
- The profit and loss statement
- Sales ledger
- Purchase ledger
- Payroll
- Accounting ratios
- Value Added Tax (VAT)
- Capital allowances
- Tax inspections and record keeping

Deciding whether you will attempt to do your own bookkeeping or whether it is worth employing a qualified accountant to do it for you is a big decision. It will depend largely on your own skills and your aptitude for the business side of things. If you have a basic knowledge of business fundamentals, and also some basic IT skills, then the accounting software available today can make it quite easy for you to do it yourself. This means you could be largely self-sufficient and keep much more up to date about just how your business is performing.

Unless you have really good accounting experience it is still a good idea to get *ad hoc* advice from an accountant. You need to ensure that you are getting things right and complying with tax regulations. You will probably need an accountant to draw up your full year-end accounts. It is very easy to miss opportunities for reducing your tax liabilities or to make mistakes in your year-end returns.

> In our first couple of years of owning a florist shop I saw an accountant every few months to check that I was doing everything I should. I particularly needed reassurance that I was making all the correct payments to the Inland Revenue and Customs & Excise. Eventually I realised that my accountant was no longer spotting anything I had missed or telling me anything I didn't already know. I then decided it was safe to stop using his services and I became completely self-sufficient.
>
> There was one particular incident that finally convinced me to stop paying an accountant. At the end of our first financial year with the

Cambridge shop I drew up a full set of year-end accounts. I then took them to my accountant to have them checked. He said everything looked fine but he couldn't understand why I hadn't included my solicitor's fees for the purchase of the business as an allowable expense. I replied that I didn't think it was allowable, but no problem. I would add it in and return a few days later with a revised profit and loss statement. When I returned he told me that since my previous visit he had decided to check out the advice he had given me. He was very sorry but he had got it wrong!

If you have set your business up as a limited company then you have to get your year-end accounts audited by an accountant. These accounts will eventually have to be filed at Companies House. If you operate as a sole trader or as a partnership you can handle all the accounting yourself. But do so only if you are certain that you know what you are doing.

The benefits of DIY accounting

If you feel confident about doing your own accounts, or perhaps a member of your family has the necessary skills and can do it for you, there are many benefits to this.

When we took over the Cambridge shop I found that the previous owners had been spending some £2,000 a year on accountant's fees, yet the information provided was minimal. It complied with the needs of the Inland Revenue and Customs & Excise and ensured that the staff were paid correctly. However, it provided almost nothing in the way of management information.

If you do your own accounting it is easy to derive a whole mine of bang up-to-date information about how your business is performing. You can examine sales trends and how well you are doing with the buying of stock. You can check that your staff costs are in line with your sales and whether all your operating expenses are under control.

On a Sunday morning I would enter all the details of our sales and purchases for the preceding week into the accounting system on my home computer. I spread the operating expenses of the business across the year and looked at what we had spent on stock in the previous week. From this it was possible to know within a few pounds how much profit we had made in the previous week. I would enter the totals in a separate spreadsheet that held our weekly sales details for every week since we took over the shop. We always aimed to beat the corresponding week from the year before and it was rare that we failed to do this. We would then look at the next week's figures from the previous year to see what we had to beat in the coming week.

I always took great pleasure from this analysis because it was usually good news and a sure indicator of how we were doing. If you are a football fan, examining the league table after your team has had a good win can be a very pleasant exercise. I found that studying the shop's statistics after a good week gave me similar pleasure.

Conversely if it is bad news then you have to look back at the week and analyse the details of the numbers to try to find the reasons. Did we get a bad deal on some stock we bought or was the weather bad perhaps? Did we have an unusually big order in the corresponding week in the previous year? These are just some of the questions you have to ask yourself.

I was often amazed when I asked other florists about how things were at the moment. They often seemed to know so little about their own business. Often people would tell me they thought that Valentine's Day was 'OK, but they didn't really know'. They would have to wait for a while – until their accountant told them. I found this incredible as I could never wait this long. If your business is not performing as it should, then you need to know in days, not in weeks or months.

Some people only realise they are paying too much for stock after months or even years. Perhaps they are not haggling enough and suppliers find them a soft touch. It could be that the prices they are paying are fine but their wastage is far too high – and that might be because they simply buy too much. It may be because they are not cleaning buckets and vases well enough or because they have not invested in a dosing unit. Whatever the reason you have to know very quickly that there is a problem. You have to find the cause and see what action you can take to fix it.

The benefits of DIY accounting? Checklist

✓ Take initial advice from a qualified accountant.
✓ Learn how to keep your own day-to-day accounts. Your local Business Link offers regular training days on accounting and financial planning.
✓ Keep records of previous years' accounts accessible.

Drawing up budgets and targets

I have always found that a good dose of pessimism helps you take a realistic stance when you make financial predictions about the future. Assume that there will be unforeseen problems and setbacks. Then when things do go wrong, as they inevitably do, you may still be able to achieve your targets and make an acceptable profit. I learned a lot from all my years in the computer world that subsequently helped us in our floristry ventures. We all learn lessons from history and our own experiences in life – what we got right and what we got wrong, how we could have done things differently to avoid the problems. Past experiences will also help to mould your general approach and attitude to how you run your business.

When I worked for a large American computer manufacturer I was responsible for running the education and training part of their business across Northern Europe. I had a track record over many years of consistently beating my sales and profit targets. This was not because I was particularly clever. It was mostly because I managed to tone down the wildly ambitious aims of senior management. I worked very hard to negotiate my targets down to more realistic, achievable levels. I was amazed that my American peers were so keen to please that they would agree to huge targets that were simply unachievable.

I had several years of regularly travelling to head office in Silicon Valley to deliver good financial results. The board then decided it would be a good idea if I moved over there and turned around the ailing US part of the business. The package on offer was very tempting, with a much larger salary, two company cars (one for me and one for Liz) and all sorts of other benefits. Liz came out and we spent a week looking at houses and schools in the San José area.

The problem was that they wanted me to take an ailing business, with annual turnover of just over $20 million. I was expected to grow this to nearly $60 million in three years. I knew this was absolutely impossible. I felt that a lot of my success in Europe was down to luck. I had some great people working for me and we benefited from a very healthy customer base. The situation in the US was much harder and the competition tougher.

I did entertain the thought of accepting the job, taking the money on offer and simply accepting that the objectives were impossible. I knew I would face the prospect of three years of missing targets, though. I would have to take all the flak that went with this, and eventually would get fired for failing to deliver. Financially this would mean an excellent pay off but I just had to turn it down.

I had frequently sat in the boardroom and seen other senior managers taken apart in merciless fashion for failing to 'make the numbers'. I had no desire to be on the receiving end of this. It really is like being thrown to the lions and I had seen the effect it had on some of my peers.

As the owner of a florist shop you do not have to suffer the angst of trying to explain poor results to senior management. However, you do need to be able to explain it to yourself, therefore you should be honest and realistic. Develop plans as if your livelihood depends on it – because it probably does!

It is essential for any business to have realistic sales targets to aim for. You need a budget, with money for contingencies built in, for all the purchases and operating expenses. Very importantly you also need a sensible aim for the year-end net profit.

I have met florists who do none of this. They take the view that customers will either buy or they won't, and there is little they can do to affect this. There are costs they have to incur and they will try to be very careful what they spend and they hope they will make enough of a profit to live. This is no way to run a business and I've never met anyone who operates in this way whom I would regard as successful. Some of the best-known designer florists in the UK admit their business was a financial disaster in the early days. It was only when they realised that they had to get a grip on all the business issues that they became a financial success.

If you do not have sales targets you have nothing to aim for. If you do not have a budget you have nothing to measure your expenditure against.

Sales targets can be estimated by taking the shop's previous year's actual sales, comparing this with preceding years, and figuring out the trends. You should try to quantify what you plan to do in the next year that will boost sales further. Think about how sales might be affected by your competitors, local circumstances and the economic forecasts for the country as a whole. You should be ambitious but realistic.

You should be absolutely confident in your own mind that the sales target is achievable. Setting unrealistically high targets can be demoralising when you consistently fail to meet them. Meeting or exceeding the targets will give you a real buzz.

If you need to raise finance from the bank you may draw up targets and budgets that you believe will impress the bank manager. He will dissect the numbers and if he sees that your optimism greatly outweighs your realism, he will deem you a bad risk. You have to produce numbers that you can justify and demonstrate that there is sufficient contingency for when things go wrong.

The budget for buying stock and paying for all the other operating expenses can also be calculated by examining previous years. You then factor in all of the expected increases. Some of these will be known and some you will simply have to increase by the expected rate of inflation. Some will be affected by your own plans for making changes to the business. I always then add another small percentage to allow for the unforeseen extra costs that always occur in reality.

I love to watch TV programmes featuring people starting a new business or developing an old property. It is usually fascinating to see their lack of planning and their incredible optimism. You witness their angst when everything inevitably goes horribly wrong with huge cost overruns and missed deadlines. As the saying goes, 'If you fail to plan, you plan to fail'.

If you have no historical data, because you are starting up a new business, this is more difficult. You will have to identify all the expected costs and calculate a budget that includes a good measure of contingency. New businesses usually greatly underestimate the costs involved. It is a good idea to draw up the first budget with an accountant and someone who has real experience of owning a florist shop. If you only talk to an accountant you will not learn enough. There are all sorts of costs for a florist that the typical accountant is unaware of. You can often learn far more from an experienced shop owner.

Drawing up budgets and targets? Checklist

✓ Set yourself realistic targets.
✓ Keep a firm grip on your budget.
✓ Historical data are vital: do not neglect to maintain records.
✓ Talk to other experienced shop owners.

The profit and loss statement

There are a whole range of low cost, easy to learn and easy to use software packages available to make your accounting relatively straightforward. You can set up the details of your suppliers, account customers and the different classes of sales and expenses. Once you get used to using the system it is easy to spend a few minutes at the end of each day entering all the transactions for that day. Alternatively a couple of hours at the end of the week is all it takes to enter all of the details for that week.

With a few clicks of a mouse you can look at all your sales, stock purchases and operating expenses. This can be displayed graphically to show weekly, monthly, quarterly and annual totals. You can look at bar charts and graphs showing these totals and examine the trends. You can find out exactly what you have spent with each supplier and what each account customer has spent. Completing your quarterly VAT return can be done in minutes.

Regardless of when your financial year is, it is possible at any time to get the system to give you an approximate profit and loss statement for the past twelve months' trading. The only time many florists get to see a profit and loss statement is when their accountant draws it up at year-end. This is usually several months after the end of the shop's financial year. The problem with this is that when you come to examine it you are looking at old information. All sorts of aspects of your business may have changed drastically in the past few months. By the time you realise that trends have changed and there are problems that need addressing urgently, you could already have wasted much time and money.

A typical profit and loss statement for a healthy florist shop might look similar to the example on page 104. This shows actual financial results for the last three years and also the targets and budgets for the current year.

Sales ledger

Accounting software will easily maintain a comprehensive sales ledger system. This is the modern equivalent of the old double entry bookkeeping method. It enables you to see every order placed by every customer, the payments they have made and what they currently owe. At the click of a

Profit and loss statement for Apex Florist

	Budget 2004–05	Actual 2003–04	Actual 2002–03	Actual 2001–02
Sales				
cash	49258	45008	37577	34379
cheques	9122	8688	9698	7262
credit cards	187220	178305	159491	152909
relay	51475	51475	58731	55949
on account	35185	31987	23590	17382
TOTAL	332260	315463	289087	267881
Cost of sales				
opening stock	5497	5103	5046	4475
purchases (relay)	66975	66975	65914	61667
purchases (stock)	115913	108433	91572	84458
less closing stock	–5497	–5497	–5103	–5046
TOTAL	182888	175014	157429	145554
GROSS PROFIT	149372	140449	131658	122327
Other income				
bank interest	150	130	84	23
	150665	140579	131742	122350
Overheads				
advertising	5117	4609	3234	2868
bank charges	495	492	372	199
credit card charges	2350	2234	1929	1766
cleaning & misc.	1050	1031	1039	1017
sundries	30	31	12	55
travel & subsistence	350	163	48	249
IT	480	743	1342	818
insurance	650	626	574	566
staff welfare	395	380	370	467
light & heat	1045	990	831	876
motor expenses	8423	7921	5475	3628
print, post, stationery	700	672	485	447
rent	18000	17654	16375	14715
subs, books, training	400	181	37	25
telephone	2250	1784	2062	1856
prof. fees	30	209	1103	1813
wages	62139	57013	54461	49363
repairs & renewals	1100	1969	810	398
rates & water	7550	7354	7682	7915
TOTAL	112554	106056	98241	89041
Depreciation				
furniture & fittings	753	966	1243	1604
motor vehicles	1138	1517	2022	2698
TOTAL	1891	2483	3265	4302
Total operating costs	114445	108539	101506	93343
Trading profit	35077	32040	30236	29007

NB: all figures are exclusive of VAT

mouse it can show the average number of days each individual customer takes to pay invoices.

You can create professional invoices and statements. Again, at the click of the mouse you can look at every unpaid invoice that is more than thirty days overdue. You can examine how much each customer has spent in total over the past year and then compare this with previous years.

This is a crucial aspect of any business as it is so important to the cash flow. It is no good clocking up lots of sales on account if you are not promptly invoicing customers and ensuring they pay as quickly as possible. Many businesses are very slow to pay their bills. Unfortunately many of them perceive this to be good business practice because it is beneficial to their cash flow.

Many large businesses with healthy cash surpluses will not pay supplier invoices for three months or more, regardless of the stated terms of payment on the invoice. So even though you might clearly state that your terms are 30 days net many businesses will take no notice of this. After polite reminders you may decide to get tough with them and try charging them interest. Unfortunately, this will not cut any ice and they may well drop you as a supplier.

Some customers will just sit on any invoice that does not meet their exact requirements as they see this as justification for not paying it. Invoices need to specify accurately the details of each order. This should include the exact name and address of the business or person placing the order, the name of the recipient of the flowers, a description of the order, the delivery date, amount and often a purchase order number. Some large businesses will want separate invoices for each different department of their organisation that may have ordered flowers. Some want a separate invoice for each and every order. If you do not comply with their preferences they will simply delay payment until you do.

In Cambridge I found that private individuals, the University colleges, and most small businesses paid their bills very promptly. We had some very large companies who were consistently slow payers but they always paid eventually. I gave up trying to make them pay more quickly. Any problems we experienced with getting any invoice paid almost always related to an admininstrative problem, rather than any deliberate attempt to avoid payment.

Purchase ledger

This is very similar to the sales ledger but contains information about your suppliers. It records the details of every invoice they have sent you, the payments you have made and any outstanding balances. It is an easy way to see how much you spend with each individual supplier and to compare how much you spend on stock each week, quarter and year. You can also compare the ratios of stock purchase to sales, which is of crucial importance to your profitability. We would study these ratios every month and review what we thought of the deal we were currently getting from each of the wholesalers and whether we needed to take any action.

> One month we suspected that one of our largest suppliers, whom we had been using for years, was starting to do some opportunistic overcharging. We rang around other local shops that we knew used the same supplier and compared notes with them. We established that they were indeed overcharging us and a letter of complaint was immediately faxed to them. This detailed our complaints and threatened them with the permanent loss of all our business. Their response was a sizeable one-off credit against our next invoice, lower prices and price lists faxed to us the day before each future visit.

It is a source of frustration for many shops that often a new wholesaler operating in their area will start by offering excellent services, prices and quality but that over time their performance gradually slides. You have to study the messages in your purchase ledger system to be able to identify quickly when this starts to happen.

Payroll

It is possible to calculate staff wages and make appropriate payments to your employees and the Inland Revenue, simply by using the documentation available from the Inland Revenue itself. They provide guidance books, together with tax and National Insurance tables. They also send out regular updates to notify you of any changes to tax codes and bandwidths that result from the Chancellor's annual budget. This may be all you need if you only have one or two employees but if you have several then I would recommend a more automated method. Either use your accountant or acquire a software package such as Sage Instant Payroll. The latter is a very cost-effective solution as, for an outlay of some £100 per year, Sage will supply an excellent system.

Sage is an easy to learn package that will handle your regular payroll and all the month-end and year-end processes. Every time there is any change in legislation or tax codes and rates, etc., you will receive a CD that keeps your system up to date. The software is very easy to use and, if you have any problems, the Sage help desk service is excellent.

If you use Sage Accounts for all your general accounting there is a link from Sage Payroll that will automatically transfer all the payroll data straight into your accounts.

Every month you have to make the appropriate payment to the Inland Revenue for income tax and national insurance. Payroll software will calculate all the complexities of tax credits and maternity benefit, etc. to ensure you make the correct payments.

You can pass all the information about your staff and their hours to an accountant who will do all the work for you but I would recommend anyone at least to look at payroll software packages first. They are so easy to use and can save you so much money. Once I became used to using Sage Payroll I found it took me approximately an hour to do all the work necessary to pay eight employees each fortnight. Using an online banking system the net pay was transferred directly to each employee's bank account. The month-end tax and National Insurance return took an extra ten minutes and the year-end processes took less than half a day.

Accounting ratios

You can keep a tight rein on your stock costs and other expenses by regularly examining certain ratios. The most important one, which has already been covered to some extent in chapter 2, is the gross profit in relation to total sales.

You need to look at the total amount spent on stock in relation to the total sales for all the orders that are actually fulfilled by your shop. By this I mean taking account of the incoming relay orders that you execute but discounting the relay orders that you send for execution by another shop.

Thus you are examining the real cost of what you have to buy to fulfil all of your orders, including all the wastage. This ratio will vary from shop to shop but will usually work out to be in the region of 50 per cent.

Some shops are advertised for sale boasting some very impressive gross profit percentages but often this just reflects the way the owners have chosen to present their accounts. You need to examine exactly how they have accounted for all the sales and purchases. Only when you know how they have accounted for their relay orders can you determine the real gross profit.

Once you know what the average is over a period of time when the shop is performing well and meeting your net profit targets, then you should aim to maintain this ratio at a similar level. Any creeping above the norm should be taken as a warning sign. You should examine why this is happening so that you can take action to get your profitability back on track.

It is also a good idea to monitor the ratio of all the other operating expenses over which you have a level of control. You cannot do anything about the rent once you have signed the lease but the amount spent on wages and advertising is very much your decision. We found that the percentage we spent on wages grew steadily but there were good reasons for this. We wanted to reward the staff properly for all their good work and as we got older we wanted to have more leisure time for ourselves.

From talking to other shops and to business transfer agents, who have experience of selling many florist shops, we knew that we employed one florist more than the norm for our level of sales. We were comfortable with this as it was our choice. We wanted to know for sure that we could get each day's orders made up and delivered well before 5pm, no matter how busy the day had been. Some florists operate with the absolute minimum staff. On a busy day they are still delivering orders well into the evening and possibly turning away some late orders. This can maximise profits and, in a shop struggling to keep its head above water financially, it may be essential.

We always knew that this situation might be forced upon us if times were bad. While we were making a good profit we much preferred to live with an above average wages bill. We were sometimes overstaffed on a quiet day but it meant we could still cope relatively comfortably with all the very busy days.

Watching the advertising spend and keeping to your budget are also very important. You may be tempted to opt for a larger colour advertisement when the Yellow Pages rep makes their annual visit. If you are, you need to think long and hard about what difference this might make. Make your best estimate of how many extra calls you are likely to receive and then do your sums. Do not simply believe what the rep tells you.

An initiative from the British Florist Association, working with the Centre for Interfirm Comparison, has resulted in a benchmarking service called FloriBest. For a cost of some £120 you supply them with the details of your sales and costs. In return they will send you a report showing how you compare with similar florists. This enables you to see how you rate with regard to gross and net profits, sales per employee, average order values, sales per square foot and much other useful information. If enough florists sign up to this service it will prove enormously beneficial to the industry.

Value Added Tax (VAT)

If you do your books manually the quarterly VAT return can be a nightmare but if you use accounting software it can be done in minutes. For the purposes of this book I have assumed that all shops are now registered for VAT. The current threshold means that any business with annual sales exceeding £58,000 will have to register for VAT. There can be very few businesses smaller than this unless it is the first year of trading for a new start up venture.

Accounting software can strip out all the VAT from your accounts for the purposes of producing a profit and loss statement. It will also ensure it is all correctly accounted for and that the right amounts are paid to Customs & Excise at the right time.

To claim the VAT back on any purchases made you need to ensure that you have a VAT invoice or a proper VAT receipt. This should state the actual items purchased, not just the amount spent. A VAT inspector will want evidence that the items purchased really were items you can realistically use within your business. A till receipt that does not specify the item purchased, even though it may have a VAT number on it, will not satisfy an inspector.

Although most items are subject to the standard rate of VAT (currently 17.5 per cent), the fuel rate for electricity and gas is only 5 per cent. Some items are liable to VAT, some are not and some require checking in the

VAT guides supplied. For example, if you take all the staff out for a Christmas dinner you can reclaim half of any VAT element in the bill.

Capital allowances

Items of a capital nature bought for the business cannot be deducted directly from the profits. Instead you receive capital allowances on the expenditure. The rates of allowance in the first year are as follows:

- 40 per cent on plant and machinery, but not motor cars;
- 100 per cent for new low-emission cars for use by you or your staff, in the business;
- 25 per cent for other cars but for cars costing more than £12,000 the maximum allowance is £3,000.

In subsequent years, the balance of expenditure is written down by 25 per cent on a reducing-balance basis.

Tax inspections and record keeping

I have had a visit from an Inland Revenue inspector to ensure that I was handling everything correctly in relation to the payroll. This focused on whether I was paying the correct amounts due for income tax and National Insurance. This proved to be no problem as I was able to satisfy the inspector easily by demonstrating that I knew how to calculate the payroll either manually or by using a software package.

Everything relating to the payroll was filed and when the inspector randomly requested certain information it was easy to find. If your paperwork is in a mess the inspector will not be impressed. If it takes a long time to find something you are much more likely to have a prolonged and more detailed visit.

After Liz had owned her first shop for about eighteen months we had a full VAT inspection. I was given due warning and as most of the shop paperwork was stored in the office in our home they agreed to visit the house, rather than the shop. Two inspectors spent almost a complete day with me going through the accounts and my VAT returns in great detail. I kept them well supplied with tea and biscuits but it was obvious that no matter how friendly and helpful I was, they were still going to do a very detailed inspection.

I found they concentrated very much on everything related to all the relay orders that had come in and out via Teleflorist. They had found from experience that it was in applying the information from the relay service provider that florist shops were most likely to make mistakes. This did not surprise me as in the early days both my accountant and myself were very confused by the guidance given. I eventually had to talk to the Teleflorist accounts department to clarify things.

When we later became Interflora members I found their finance handbook was excellent. This is also a subject well covered in the classroom on their new members courses.

Again I found the inspectors were clearly impressed that I could readily show them details they asked for. This was accomplished by either finding an answer within the computerised accounting system or by pulling an appropriate piece of paper out of a file.

Following the inspection they sent me a report stating that there was one area where they believed I had made mistakes. They stated that I owed Customs & Excise just over a hundred pounds but I was sure they had made a mistake. I contested this and after a few letters went back and forth they finally accepted that we did not owe them anything.

Some two years after we took over the Cambridge shop I received another telephone call from Customs & Excise. They wanted to ask me some questions over the phone. It was evident that if I could not provide satisfactory answers I would probably receive a personal visit. Thankfully I found them perfectly pleasant and helpful once I could convince them I was processing everything related to VAT correctly. This thirty-minute telephone call was a big improvement on a full day's inspection. I believe they make more initial checks by telephone now because of manpower constraints.

It can be a real nuisance having to keep records for six years. I will be very glad when I can finally dispose of all the archive boxes in my loft. However, when you have an inspection I can assure you it all seems worthwhile. If the inspectors want to see paperwork you need to be able to find it. If you do not have it, or you cannot find it, then they will become even more diligent. This is likely to be bad news financially.

8 Staff

This chapter looks at:

- Recruitment
- The florist's skill set
- Staffing at peak periods
- Creativity and speed
- How many staff do you need?
- Training and qualifications
- Driver skills

- Terms and conditions
- Hiring and firing
- Trust and cooperation
- Communicating with staff
- Measuring productivity
- Business trends at peak periods
- Health and safety

The floristry trade asks a tremendous amount of the people it employs and yet the financial compensation can be very meagre. I was always amazed by the wide range of skills we looked for each time we employed a new florist. Yet somehow we did find people with a very broad skill set who worked extremely hard, showed us great loyalty and were a joy to work with.

In my time in the IT industry I found that to hire the sort of people I needed was very expensive. It often meant paying them a basic salary of some £40,000 plus and providing them with a BMW, all their petrol expenses (business and private), private health cover and a host of other benefits. When I moved to the world of floristry I found that to fit in with the industry norms we were paying people only a few pounds an hour. However, we still had to insist upon all sorts of different skills and attributes.

It is unfortunately a fact of life that most jobs that people really like to do will not pay high wages. Thus florists are usually motivated to do work they really enjoy, even though they could earn much the same stacking shelves in a supermarket. We always tried to provide the best wages and conditions that we could but to stay competitive in retail floristry there is a limit to how far you can go. The higher your wages bill, the smaller your profits. A high wages bill also reduces the price you can ask if your business is put up for sale.

Recruitment

New staff can often be found without spending anything on advertising. If you let your visiting wholesalers know that you need an extra florist they will spread the word at all the other shops they visit. If there is a local college running floristry courses they can be a good source of trainees. We had some success with simply putting a notice in the shop window. When all else failed we placed a small classified advertisement in the local paper and this always attracted some suitable applicants.

The general reputation of your shop will have a big impact on whether you receive applications from experienced local florists. If you have a reputation as a good employer, paying fair wages, recruitment will obviously be much easier. Some shops are continually advertising for staff. This makes the pool of local florists very wary of the reasons why their staff turnover is so high. Again, the wholesalers' grapevine effectively spreads the word about which shops have happy staff and which do not to all the local shops.

When interviewing florists you should obviously check their previous experience and qualifications and take up references. Telephoning a previous employer will reveal far more then a written reference. Because of all the legislation in place today most employers are reluctant to be at all negative in a written reference. A telephone call may well reveal that the applicant had a poor attendance and punctuality record or was unpopular with their colleagues.

It is also a good idea to set a timed test for making up one or two products. A lot of otherwise experienced florists are slow in their make-up work. Someone who works slowly will prove frustrating and expensive. The productivity of your other staff may also slacken as they question why they are working so quickly in comparison to the newcomer.

Recruiting staff? Checklist

✓ It may not be necessary to advertise for new staff. Use word of mouth and a notice in the shop itself.

✓ A classified ad in a local paper will usually bring a large response.

✓ Always take up references. Phone rather than write to referees.

✓ Consider a timed test for recruits.

The florist's skill set

When I first came to compile a list of the skills we wanted from a florist I was amazed at how long and diverse the list was. Apart from wanting people who had both the design skills and the technical make-up skills essential for a competent florist, we wanted so much more. A florist needs to have excellent sales skills, both over the phone and with customers actually present in the shop. She needs IT skills to enable her to use the computer for sending and receiving relay orders and to be able to word process letters and price quotations for customers. She needs to be physically strong enough to be on her feet nearly all day and to condition stock and carry full buckets and vases around.

Her use of English has to be good enough to take and send orders around the world without spelling mistakes. A basic knowledge of world geography is also very useful when sending relay orders. Her customer service skills will be tested to the limit when handling difficult customers and the very strange complaints you inevitably receive in a florist shop.

And looking after distraught relatives when they come to place an order for funeral flowers requires exactly the right balance of sympathy and selling.

Staffing at peak periods

At peak times incredible levels of stamina are required to work long hours at a very fast pace. I have previously mentioned the pressures I saw people exposed to in the IT industry. This does not compare with the sort of pressures that staff are subject to in a busy florist shop on Valentine's Day. This will be hard to believe for anyone who has not experienced it personally.

On a typical Valentine's Day we would start very early after just a couple of hours sleep. We would then work non-stop all day and well into the evening with no breaks. We even found it difficult to find the time to visit the lavatory. We used all the labour we could find – extra florists and drivers and also general dogsbodies who could keep us supplied with food and drink while we worked. I have never experienced anything quite like it in terms of hard work and pressure.

At peak periods staffing can be much easier if you have a number of staff who are prepared to work full-time in a peak week, even if they are usually part-time. We employed people who worked anything from two to six days in a normal week. They were all able to work a full week at peak times and this made staffing so much easier. Trying to find extra experienced florists for just a few days can be very difficult.

Another ability most employers require of their staff is for them to be proactive rather than reactive. These words may seem overused but they relate to two very different personalities. Proactive people generally make things happen while reactive people have things happen to them. For example, assume that two different florists are given an order for a bouquet of lilies required for a formal presentation at a function that day. The problem is that all the available lilies are tight and unlikely to open for several days. The proactive florist will call the customer and explain this and make alternative suggestions. The reactive florist will go ahead and use the tight lilies and hope there will not be a complaint.

You need staff who will think ahead about anything that could result in a complaint and take corrective action to avoid potential problems. If the day starts slowly with few orders, assume that it will not last. Get the orders made up early and assume that lots more will flood in all through the day. Taking it easy early in the day can so easily rebound on you. It is much better to crack on with the work and then ease off later if it does turn out to be a quiet day.

Creativity and speed

There are many people who can take a selection of cut flowers and make them into a beautiful arrangement or a bouquet. Retail floristry means having to do this at speed. Something that might be made in an hour in a flower arranger's club will often have to be made in a few minutes in a shop.

The labour cost involved in making whatever your customers order is a vitally important aspect of a shop making a profit or running at a loss. It is no good having the most talented designers in the world if they take too long on the make-up work. Experienced florists can put together gift-wrapped bouquets in a few minutes. Hand-tied bouquets are usually made in 10–15 minutes and arrangements in oasis in perhaps 15–20 minutes or fewer, depending on the size.

Obviously increased speed usually comes with experience. However, there are people with a good eye for design and with a good knowledge of flowers who never achieve the productivity levels needed in a shop.

How many staff do you need?

The number of staff you need will depend very much on the people themselves and the nature of work in a particular shop. I have seen florists who can make up an average of six orders per hour and others who struggle to achieve half that. Most florists increase their speed and productivity with experience but some reach a certain level that they find very difficult to improve on.

I often found that an order that was being made up could suddenly become urgent. Perhaps the customer had arrived early to collect it, parked on a double yellow line and wanted us to hurry. It was interesting to observe how the florist handled the situation. Some could put a spurt on and complete the work easily. Some would become all fingers and thumbs and the make-up could go horribly wrong.

If you have a small shop with annual sales of less than £100,000 then on an average day all the make-up work could be done by just one fast, experienced florist. The problem is that you also need to serve customers in the shop, answer the phone and buy and condition stock. This will mean you really need a second person to make the deliveries. Thus it is possible to manage in a small shop with just two staff. Of course this still means that you will have to find extra cover for holidays and peak periods.

With annual sales of between £150,000 to £250,000 you will probably need three to four staff for an average week, including a driver. A large shop with sales in excess of £300,000 will typically need five staff.

As turnover increases, the wage bill, as a percentage of your sales, should decrease. Thus a small shop with sales of just £80,000 will probably need two staff. A medium-sized shop turning over some £240,000 will probably manage with a total of four staff. A large shop with sales of perhaps £330,000 can manage with five staff.

Sales per employee can vary from as little as £40,000 in a small shop to over £65,000 in a large shop. This makes a huge difference to the profitability and is one of the reasons why it is impossible to make much profit from a small shop. Very large shops, with sales in excess of £500,000, can find they reach a size where sales per employee start to fall off slightly. When there are lots of staff the productivity per employee will usually decline as each staff member feels under less pressure. There are exceptions to this where the management control is very good and the staff motivation is kept high.

Training and qualifications

Much of the training given to people employed as florists is hands-on in the shop with an experienced and competent florist demonstrating how to make up the different products and then helping the trainee to copy them.

Liz would set objectives for a trainee. They had not just to make things to an acceptable standard, but they had to do it within set time limits. This very practical training can dovetail with formal part-time college courses. Usually these lead to NVQs in Floristry at Levels 2 and 3. Many students of floristry will attend college and volunteer to work for a local shop to gain practical experience.

Alternatively there are part-time and full-time courses leading to a nationally recognised qualification. These courses include:

- BTEC First Diploma in Floristry. There are no particular entry qualifications needed for this one-year course although some GCSEs/S grades or their equivalent would help.
- BTEC National Diploma in Floristry. This is a two-year course that usually requires four GCSEs (A-C)/S grades (1-3), a BTEC first award or Intermediate GNVQ/GSVQ level 2, or the appropriate SQA modules or their equivalent.
- BTEC Higher National Diploma in Floristry. This is a two- or three-year course that prepares people for managerial work or self-employment. It usually requires five GCSEs (A-C)/S grades (1-3) with one A level/Advanced Higher/two Higher grades, or a relevant BTEC national diploma. Other alternative entry requirements are appropriate SQA modules or equivalent, such as vocational A level/GSVQ level 3.

Experienced florists can gain the Intermediate Certificate for the Society of Floristry.

The examinations for this are tough and cover theoretical and practical aspects of floristry. The pass rate is very low because the marking is so strict.

Liz took and passed the ICSF and I remember how elated she was when she received her results. I know that she rated this qualification really highly. It involved having to select appropriate flowers and utilise both design and technical skill in the make-up work. It also imposed very tough time limits that related to the real world of working in a shop. This helped her gradually to build up her productivity levels until she could work through a large batch of varied orders in very quick time.

Liz had planned to move on from the ICSF level to take the National Diploma for the Society of Floristry (NDSF), which is the highest qualification in the UK and is internationally recognised. However, the pressures of running such a busy shop meant that she had to postpone it. I know she was sad that she never found the time to get round to it. It was a qualification she had always greatly respected.

The staff took their lead from Liz as everyone realised that productivity was supremely important to the overall profitability of the shop. We could not afford to employ people who would spend ages looking at an arrangement they were working on and then deciding it was not quite right and starting again. This can happen for a large, complex arrangement or perhaps for a tricky bridal bouquet but the typical order must be produced quickly. It always amused us when customers remarked that it must be lovely to be paid for playing with flowers all day.

The Society of Floristry is open to all professional florists. It helps its members to contact each other and find information on all sorts of books, training and events related to the industry. It is possible to be a student member if you are studying floristry and to then progress to full membership (MSF) on passing the ICSF exams. Further progression to become a Fellow (FSF) is achieved by passing the NDSF exams.

At the time of writing, the government has plans for introducing a new apprenticeship scheme. This will provide on-the-job training for would-be florists as young as 14. The planned reforms will lead to:

- Young Apprenticeships – for 14–16 year olds, these provide the opportunity to spend up to two days a week in a shop learning a trade;
- Pre-Apprenticeship – based upon the Entry to Employment scheme for people who can demonstrate potential but are not ready to enter an Apprenticeship;
- Apprenticeship – this scheme would replace the Foundation Modern Apprenticeship;
- Advanced Apprenticeship – this would replace the Advanced Modern Apprenticeship and will equal two good A levels.

The new scheme would open up Apprenticeship opportunities to adults, scrapping the previous 25-year-old age limit.

Driver skills

When hiring drivers previous experience of delivery work is always preferable. You also need someone who knows the area really well. Maps are no substitute for local knowledge. Drivers unfamiliar with the area will waste lots of time referring to maps and getting lost.

Some people think that if you can drive, you can deliver, but there is more to delivery driving than that. Experienced delivery drivers do not simply know their way around. They know which routes to take at different times of day. They make allowances for school times and avoid known bottlenecks.

Experienced drivers also know that you cannot always park correctly and legally when dropping off an order. They are streetwise enough to know what they can get away with to avoid problems and keep to deadlines. To make deliveries these days in city centres, without ever infringing any regulations, would take for ever.

A driver needs to be clean and smart and confident enough to make appropriate small talk with the recipient and must be careful to avoid any damage to the product that is being delivered.

For insurance purposes you ideally want someone over the age of 25 and with a full clean licence.

Terms and conditions

I have already stated that the floristry profession is very poorly paid for the skills required. We paid a basic hourly rate that varied from £6.30 to £7.45, dependent on experience and ability. This may seem low, but we were known to be one of the highest payers in the Cambridge area. These rates were certainly well above the national average for florists.

For overtime outside normal shop hours we paid 1.5 times the standard rate. Staff received four weeks' paid holiday a year and we also paid them for all bank holidays. Many shops pay just a standard rate, however many hours their staff work. And some only include bank holidays as part of the annual holiday entitlement.

At the time of writing the statutory adult minimum wage is £4.85 per hour. Many proprietors struggle to pay much more than this and stay in profit.

Delivery drivers typically earn a lower wage than florists, more like £5 per hour. This is because there are always so many people looking for driving jobs. Our 15-year-old Saturday girl was paid £4 per hour and her work represented excellent value.

Hiring and firing

New members of staff must have a contract. This should state their rate of pay, the hours they will be expected to work, holiday entitlement, details of sickness pay and the period of notice due for termination. Both the proprietor and employee need to sign this document and each must retain a copy.

In the event of unsatisfactory performance you have to follow the correct disciplinary procedures to ensure you do not leave yourself open to a charge of unfair dismissal. The propensity of 'no win, no fee' services promoted these days has encouraged many people to seek financial compensation, often regardless of the real reasons relating to why they have lost their job.

If you make someone redundant you have to put them 'at risk' first. This means telling them their job is not secure and consulting fully with them before any notice of termination is given.

If an employee is upset by banter between their workmates, you have to take action to stop this. There is always a lot of banter in a shop and much of it is inevitably of a sexual nature. I've never been aware of anyone being offended by this. I often found myself the only man in the shop, working with up to eight women. It was much like working with men and the jokes were as blue as any I have heard elsewhere. I was always pleased that the girls felt comfortable enough with me around not to feel the need to change their usual behaviour.

When the girls went on holiday they would often send a racy postcard (usually showing a nude man) back to the shop. So that I didn't feel left out they would send me one showing a nude woman. All of these postcards went up on the workroom notice board and nobody was ever offended.

However, some people can be offended by this sort of thing and if this is the case you must take action. Any cases of sexual harassment that end up in court are likely to be found in favour of the plaintiff.

Employees need to know that if they have a grievance they can talk to their manager about it. The details of the grievance, and any agreed action, should be carefully documented.

An employee who is being disciplined, and is a member of a union, has the right to be accompanied by a union representative at any disciplinary hearing. Even if an employee is caught stealing, and admits to it, instant dismissal is not possible. The disciplinary process must still take place.

If an employee wants to work flexible hours, perhaps because they have young children, and this does not fit in with your plans, there is a strict procedure to follow in dealing with the issue. Parents have many rights these days and the law expects employers to be sympathetic to their needs.

As an employer you should keep a separate personnel file for the routine information you hold on each employee. The Data Protection Act requires that highly sensitive data, such as doctors' certificates produced for absence, should be kept separately.

Hiring and firing? Checklist

✓ All new staff must be given a contract.
✓ Always follow the correct disciplinary procedure.
✓ Document grievances and any agreed action carefully.
✓ Keep a separate personnel file for each employee.

Trust and cooperation

We have covered some of the aspects relating to the regulations for unsatisfactory performance. I have always found that the usual relationship between employee and employer in a florist shop is much more likely to be one of trust and friendship.

It is very easy for anyone handling direct customer sales to pocket cash occasionally instead of ringing it up and putting it in the till. In a florist shop it can be very difficult to catch anyone doing this. If it is a transaction that has an order form related to it, there will be an audit trail. This enables you to check that it has been paid and accounted for. In fact this is an essential task at the end of the day to ensure that all the orders have been paid for. It is very easy on a busy day to forget to put an order received over the phone through the credit card machine.

However, when a customer dashes into the shop for £10-worth of cut flowers and slaps a £10 note on the counter before dashing out again, this can be a tempting opportunity for anyone who is not totally honest.

We were very lucky in employing people we trusted completely. By treating your staff fairly and rewarding them well you are more likely to build up two-way trust and friendship with your staff.

The only time we have ever doubted anyone we employed was some years ago. We found that the till was often £10 or £20 short at the end of the day. By studying which members of staff were in the shop on days when the till was short, we narrowed the numbers down to two possible suspects. The problem was that the till was only ever short on days when both these staff were present. We suspected that the culprit did this deliberately so that we would not be able to pinpoint one individual. The problem was eventually solved when both employees left of their own accord and from that day the till was never noticeably short again.

In the Cambridge shop we built a team of florists whom we trusted 100 per cent. All of them were good customers as well as employees and would take advantage of the twenty per cent staff discount we gave them. They were all so scrupulously honest that when they paid for anything they would ask a colleague to ring it up on the till. They always wanted to be seen to be making the correct payment.

The shop closed officially at 5pm each day but often we would have late customers. This often meant that one of the girls could not leave until 5.30pm. I would always thank them for staying late and promise to add half an hour's overtime to their pay but they would often tell me not to bother. You are unlikely to get this sort of commitment unless you reciprocate by treating the staff well. It is essential to give them the respect and recognition they deserve.

Communicating with staff

After Valentine's Day and Mother's Day Liz and I would always thank all the staff personally for the exceptionally hard work they had put in. We would also put our thanks in writing when giving them an appropriate bonus.

Communication with your staff is vital in any sort of business. Quite apart from the day-to-day chat in the shop it is important to put things in writing on a regular basis.

At the end of each month I gave each of our staff a memo summarising how the shop had performed in that month. Usually this was a 'well done' memo but if our average order value had dropped below par this was spelt out. There would be a reminder that we all had to keep working at this and ensure that we were offering a full range of prices and offering add-ons, etc. The monthly statistics provided by Interflora were also of interest to all the staff. These showed our sales, order values, comparison with the previous year and our ranking in the league table. Every month this was posted on the workroom noticeboard.

At the end of each year we would give each employee a memo summarising how the shop had performed in the past year. It also explained our aims and objectives for the coming year. I found that most employees really were interested in the broader picture. If they are properly involved they will offer many good ideas on how the business can be improved.

Employees will feel more involved in the wider world of floristry if you make relevant magazines and product and supplier brochures available to them. *The Florist & Wholesale Buyer* magazine is excellent for keeping up to date with current trends. I would also recommend *Flora* magazine and the *Focal Point* magazine from the Society of Floristry.

Measuring productivity

As I have spent most of my life working for American companies I have always been interested in cultural differences. It is interesting to analyse the differences in working methods in an American florist shop.

Often when Liz and I visited an American shop they would be happy to tell us about their working methods. Usually their staff were either 'salespeople' or 'designers'. They would be surprised to hear that in the UK it was more common for anyone working in a florist shop to be a jack-of-all-trades.

American shops tend to focus very much on developing a competitive element to all their work. It is common to see a whiteboard in the workroom showing a league table of all their designers. They track how many orders of different types are made up by each person and there are bonuses for the person topping the league each week. Often the current league leader proudly wears a 'No.1 Florist' badge. Another whiteboard will show the number of orders and the average order values for each of the salespeople. Again there are bonuses and prizes for 'achievers'.

This seems to work well over there and the typical employee will strive to be at the top of the league. However, the person at the bottom will often feel embarrassed and humiliated. The management view is that is how life should be and that it provides the required motivation for people to improve and move up the league.

Whenever I suggested implementing this sort of scheme in our shop it was resisted. I offered to put up extra money to fund the bonuses and prizes but the girls were clearly uncomfortable about this. They preferred a less competitive environment without the worry of being low down a league table. I very much wanted to do it but as the staff were so good I decided not to force this on them against their wishes. They made the valid point that such schemes could have some aspects that were counter-productive. People might be less enthusiastic to handle what looked likely to be low value orders. There could be arguments over whose turn it was to answer the phone next.

We settled on a compromise scheme that tracked the total order volumes and values. All the staff shared in equal bonuses for beating the average levels from the previous year. This worked well and the order values climbed impressively from year to year.

Business trends at peak periods

I have already mentioned the stresses and strains placed on anyone working in a florist shop at peak periods. These peaks are different both in terms of the scale of business and in the length of time the work is compressed into.

We never found Christmas a problem as there was a steady build up through December and no single day was crazily busy. We were very busy on the day the schools broke up, the last working day for most office workers and on the last couple of days before Christmas Day. However, with all the staff working a few extra hours overtime it was easily manageable.

Mother's Day was much busier but because deliveries are always spread over the Friday, Saturday and Sunday it can be quite orderly and manageable. One problem is that the range of products required for Mother's Day is very diverse. There are always lots of orders for arrangements in oasis that require longer than average make-up times. However a lot of these can be made up well in advance. With sensible forward planning this can greatly ease the pressure when it comes to the weekend.

We found that once we had a shop with Interflora membership the volume of relay orders for Mother's Day was huge. On the Thursday and Friday I would spend the entire day and well into the evening at the computer sending orders all around the world. We also received many incoming orders. The phones would be extremely busy all day long. For a new owner it can be quite scary wondering if you have both the stock and the labour to handle the volume of orders flooding in. We kept running totals of the number of different products to be made. We would regularly compare this with our historical data from previous years that told us how many we could cope with. This helped to ensure that the situation did not get out of control.

Many florists get into a terrible fix, however. By the Saturday of Mother's Day weekend we would find that many of the outgoing relay orders we sent to other florists would be rejected. This was either because they were running out of stock or because they did not have enough labour to cope with all the work. I know of one shop that had a huge batch of orders and then experienced a staffing crisis on the Saturday. This all became too much for the owners who closed the shop for good and 'did a runner'!

There were also a small number of shops that did not open on the Sunday of Mother's Day itself. This always infuriated me as there would be customer enquiries that just could not be resolved. I implored Interflora to make it a condition of membership that every participating shop should open on Mother's Day. There were of course owners who objected to Sunday opening on religious grounds.

Usually in the week before Mother's Day all the staff, including those who were part-time, would work a full week. On the Friday night we would all work until around 8pm. Saturday was always a long day with a very early start but probably finishing by around 6pm. Sunday would necessitate a very early start to get six drivers loaded up and started on the deliveries. Interflora required all orders for Sunday delivery to be delivered by 2pm but we always aimed to get them completed by 1pm to give us a bit of a safety margin.

The shop would not receive many walk-in customers on Mothering Sunday, however. By then our focus would be very much on getting all the orders out and handling enquiries.

Valentine's Day is always the biggest challenge in the florist's year. In our first few years in this industry I regarded it as a week from hell. Fortunately with experience the hell became slightly less nightmarish. People were always telling us that we must be delighted with all the money we were making on Valentine's Day. There were times when we could quite honestly have said we would have preferred less money and the opportunity to be able to handle all the business properly.

The biggest problem with Valentine's Day is the enormous volume of orders, all of which have to be delivered on the one day. This is incredibly challenging for the florists who have to make up so many orders at top speed. Finding space to store all these at a time when a shop is overflowing with stock is also a big problem. We always prayed for good weather so that we could temporarily store orders in the sheds at the back of the shop and even outside in the open air.

Valentine's Day 2004 was easier to handle because it fell on a Saturday. This always depresses sales in comparison to a weekday. It also meant that, thanks to an Interflora advertising campaign, many deliveries to recipients' work addresses were ordered for 13 February. Being able to spread the deliveries over two days made an enormous difference.

In the days leading up to Valentine's Day we would use all the skilled labour we could find. The problem was that there were simply not enough trained florists available to meet the needs of all the florist shops in the area. Consequently we always had to work long hours. Usually we could find enough extra staff to allow us to finish by around 10pm or 11pm on the night before the big day but by then everyone felt so hyperactive that it was difficult to sleep and Liz and I would be up again by 4am. The staff would arrive from around 7am and we would aim to get up to eight drivers loaded up and on the road as quickly as possible.

In the run-up to peak periods I experimented with hiring temporary telesales staff to handle the phones so that the florists could concentrate on the make-up work. This met with only limited success as it was nearly impossible for temps to learn quickly enough how to handle the many diverse orders and enquiries. Although the people we used did their very best there were errors that subsequently had to be sorted out by more experienced staff. We always hired a couple of unskilled people who would condition the stock as it was delivered. They would also clear away all the rubbish accumulating in the workroom, write out message cards and envelopes and make tea and coffee. They generally did everything they possibly could to free up the florists, so that they could concentrate on the skilled make-up work.

The end of any peak period is a good time to shift slow moving stock. People who have left their purchase until the last minute are often happy to buy just about anything if it gets them out of a hole. This is the time to sell vases and giftware that have been sitting in the shop for far too long.

Health and safety

As an employer you must provide a reasonable standard of health and safety for your own staff and also for any visitors to the shop. Health and safety inspectors have the right to enter the premises to carry out an examination and enforce legal requirements. If you have employees there are other additional rules. You must:

- inform your local authority of the business name and address;
- display the health and safety law poster in a prominent position;
- display the employer's liability insurance certificate in a prominent position;
- appoint (and provide training for) a First Aid officer.

If you have five or more employees you should also:

- produce a written statement on your policy for health and safety at work and make it available to your staff;
- assess the fire risks of the workplace and keep a written record.

To provide a safe working environment you should check that the entrances and exits are always kept clear. Fire extinguishers should be examined annually and electrical fittings and equipment checked. A full First Aid kit must be made available to all staff, together with a book for recording any accidents and action resulting from them. Chemicals have to be clearly labelled and stored safely. Appropriate protective clothing must be provided.

Your local HSE office can provide you with the following booklets, which detail the procedures you should follow to comply with the relevant legislation:

- *Health and Safety regulations: a short guide;*
- *Health and Safety law: what you should know.*

When we were inspected by the local HSE office I found them extremely helpful. They gave me good warning of their visit and I spent half a day in preparation. This mostly entailed reading the booklets and producing the necessary paperwork. They made a thorough inspection of the premises, my paperwork and posters, the First Aid kit and the fire extinguishers. The only action I had to take was to fit a chain to secure the helium bottles (for the decorative balloons) to the shop wall.

9 Deliveries

This chapter looks at:

- Scheduling deliveries
- The delivery process
- Unusual deliveries
- The cost and price of delivering
- Peak period planning

Some people think that delivery is the easy, routine part of the floristry business, the part that comes after all the difficult creative work has been done. However, every shop owner knows that delivery is a key part of the business and that it requires a lot of effort to handle efficiently and effectively.

I have often daydreamed about how nice it would be to own a business where every customer came into the shop and collected what they wanted to buy. In the floristry trade this will never happen.

Delivering can and should involve much more than the main tasks of loading up orders, calling at the right delivery addresses and handing over the flowers. I usually enjoyed making deliveries. It was an opportunity to brighten up the recipient's day and make someone happy. Also at very busy times it was nice to escape from the hustle and bustle of the shop. This is not to say that delivering is always a relaxing task. It can be anything but that when you are racing against the clock to get everything done on time.

Scheduling deliveries

At the end of each day we would write up the delivery schedule for all the orders we had for the following day. The delivery sheets were headed with the date and divided into columns with the following headings:

Sequence This was for entering the numerical sequence for each delivery based on location (address) and whether or not it was a priority delivery that had to be delivered within a particular time window.

Recipient name

Address Any address that was for a road or street name we did not recognise, or for a house with a name but no number, would be checked before leaving the shop. Finding a house by name in a long road can waste an awful lot of time.

Time required Most deliveries will be made at any time during normal working hours. Customers may pay extra for morning or afternoon delivery or to have the order delivered between particular hours.

Time of delivery We always logged an exact time of the delivery that did not look like an approximate time. For example a delivery made at 10am would be logged as either 9.59 or 10.01. We found this helped to convince a customer that you knew precisely when it was delivered!

Left at This was for the many occasions when the recipient was not in and the order had to be left with a neighbour.

One column we did not have on delivery sheets, but that I know many shops do use, was for a signature for acceptance of delivery. We decided not to ask the recipient to sign for a delivery unless the sender had requested this. While some people were happy to sign, some regarded it as an annoyance. The porters at some of the University colleges in Cambridge were often reluctant to sign for flowers. They would sometimes sign as Mickey Mouse or Donald Duck as they did not want to take responsibility if anything went wrong. Busy hospital nurses would also find it frustrating to be asked for a signature. Addenbrookes, the large teaching hospital in Cambridge, placed all kinds of restrictions on flower deliveries and many local florists felt that insisting on signatures would be the last straw that would lead them to putting a complete ban on flowers in the wards. As we delivered multiple orders there every day we could not afford to put this business at risk.

We only ever had one problem concerning signatures in all the time that we owned a shop yet the time we saved by not insisting on a signature covered the cost of correcting this single problem many times over. I know that some florists will disagree with this policy. Interflora always requested a signature but I know what worked best for us.

When we first moved to Cambridge I found navigating a strange city to make deliveries was a nightmare. I looked for a computerised solution to working out the best sequence and found a route-planner package called

ROUTE 66. I would enter all the delivery addresses and the program would print out the optimal route to take. This worked well until I reached the stage when I knew my way around well enough to do without it. Local knowledge, especially about which areas are busy at which time of day, will eventually enable you to improve on any computerised solution.

At the end of each month we filed all that month's delivery sheets. We kept these for years, as we would often receive an enquiry about deliveries we had made many months previously. Many people who send flowers are absolutely convinced that the recipient will contact them to thank them. If this does not happen they automatically assume the florist has failed to deliver. Filing delivery sheets is a quick way to deal with this frequent problem.

The delivery process

Loading deliveries onto a van is a good opportunity to double-check a number of things. I used to check that each order had all the correct attachments, such as a message card in an envelope, appropriate care cards, gold card, flower food and bow, etc. I would also look at the order to satisfy myself that it looked right. If a £30 bouquet did not look like £30 worth I would ask the florist to double-check the order and the flower content. We would invariably find that the correct value had gone into the flower content. Either the choice of flowers, or perhaps unusually high current prices, meant it looked smaller than usual. Sometimes we would decide to add more flowers to it anyway, to improve the appearance of value for money.

I believe these sorts of checks and comments are something any experienced deliverer can and should make, not just a motivated owner/driver. Obviously they need to be made tactfully and with respect for the florist who has made up the order. If the team spirit is healthy, a driver should be able to question any order they think might result in a complaint.

The driver must be very careful to protect deliveries that have to be kept upright in the van. Some drivers cut holes into thick polystyrene to slot the orders in securely. I preferred to cut holes in the top of the large cardboard boxes we received from wholesalers. I would cut some holes to fit hand-tied bouquets and some for different shaped vases. As Interflora changed their collection I would modify new boxes to fit the new products. I was subjected to a lot mickey-taking from the girls about my boxes. They wanted to know when I was going to patent my designs. At one of the shop's Christmas parties they presented me with a certificate for 'Saddest Job of the Year' for my box designs. In my defence I can only say that vases rarely fell over when I was delivering.

When handing over the flowers to the recipient I was always aware of the occasion and tried to adopt appropriate behaviour. If it was a birthday I would hand the flowers over with a big smile and wish the recipient a happy birthday. I also resorted to shameless flattery. If there was a 'Happy 50th' balloon attached I would joke that the flowers must be for the recipient's mother, as she was clearly too young. It sounds corny but it always went down well. Elderly ladies would always insist on telling me how old they were and wanted to chat at great length.

When delivering a funeral tribute the correct approach is simply to be quiet, polite and respectful. The girls would warn me when we had sympathy items to deliver to someone who had just suffered a bereavement. It is obviously not appropriate to be full of the joys of spring if the recipient is in tears.

It is often a good idea to give some very basic care advice on what to do with flowers, when handing them over. Some people think they can wait a day or two before putting flowers in water. Many people never read the care cards attached to their flowers.

It is important for the driver to have a mobile phone, as communication with the shop is often needed. The driver may need to query the delivery address. A call to the shop and a quick check on a computerised addressing system will reveal when the customer has provided the wrong house number. An order returned to the shop often means an extra journey to the correct address later in the day. If a driver is accessible through a mobile phone the staff in the shop can also tell him when *not* to deliver a particular order. Perhaps the delivery is to a remote village and another order has just come in for a further delivery to the same place. Drivers become adept at adjusting and optimising their delivery sequence to cope with events as they occur throughout the day.

Unusual deliveries

Deliveries can often be very amusing. I once had to make a delivery to a couple in a new mobile home near Cambridge. They saw me arrive and the man came to the door to warn me that there was wet cement below their door. There was a significant drop from door level to ground level and they were obviously going to build some steps on a concrete base. As he reached over to grab the bouquet his hand slipped from the door and he fell head-long into the wet cement. I helped him get up and brush the worst of the cement off his clothes. Fortunately only his pride was hurt. When I got back to the shop I checked the order to see what the card message was. It read 'Good luck in your new home'.

One customer proposed to his girlfriend by sending her red roses every day for two weeks. Each delivery was accompanied by a one-word message on a card. Only when she received the last bouquet was the message of pro-posal complete.

I remember another customer walking into the shop to ask how much our bouquets cost. When we replied that they typically ranged from £20 to £90 he said he wanted one for £100. As well as having the bouquet deliv-ered he also wanted me to deliver a diamond engagement ring. I was to phone him immediately after I had made the delivery to tell him what the recipient's reaction had been. Fortunately she was delighted and the answer was 'Yes'.

Some deliveries are not so pleasant and can present the deliverer with a tricky situation. I once delivered flowers from a distant son to his elderly mother and she broke down in tears. She told me she was suffering from depression and begged me to stay and talk to her, as she had not spoken to anyone for days. I chatted to her for as long as I could spare but had to get on with the rest of my deliveries. When I returned to the shop I contacted her son and explained what had happened. I just hoped he was able to visit her soon.

On another occasion I delivered to a lady who was absolutely terrified because a robin had flown into her house and she had a phobia about birds. She shut me in her lounge until I was able to get the bird out through the window.

I have always found that it pays to make it very clear that you are deliv-ering flowers on behalf of a florist shop. This can be done by wearing a jacket with the shop name on and by parking the sign-written shop van right outside the recipient's house. People are usually very pleased to be receiving flowers and are happy for their neighbours to know about it. And if you are delivering flowers to a woman, and her husband answers the door, you want him to know that this is not a personal delivery from you.

People can be very suspicious if they are not the sender, particularly at Valentine's Day.

One of our nicest deliveries was a bouquet for a little girl on her seventh birthday. Apparently it had always been her ambition to have flowers delivered to her. She had seen how delighted her mother was whenever she received a bouquet and she thought it was very grown up. I parked the van right outside the front door and announced that I had a special delivery for Miss Jones. Her face was a picture and it was obviously the best present she could get.

Every year we received orders from customers in the US and Canada for arrangements to be placed on relatives' graves. Most of these orders were from people who had no living relatives in our area. I felt the need to prove to them that we had correctly fulfilled their wishes. When placing the flowers on the graves I would use my digital camera to take a picture. I then either emailed this or posted it to the customer.

The delivery process is really an opportunity to add value and to represent the shop positively. You can make an impression on both the recipients and their neighbours. We have often received orders from neighbours whom we have left orders with when the designated recipient was out. They have taken flowers into their home and obviously been impressed by them and also by our delivery service. They then decided that they would use our shop.

The cost and price of delivering

The advantage of handling your own deliveries using your own staff and your own vans is that you have full control. A clean van with striking signage can be a wonderful advertisement for your shop. However at peak times you have to use other drivers as well. You may decide that delivering is a headache you would like to outsource to someone else.

In the Cambridge area I found that most courier firms that we used at peak times would charge anything between £4.50 and £6.50 for each drop around the city. However, one firm offered us a rate of just £2.50 per drop, for anywhere within about a ten-mile radius of the shop. This was so incredibly cheap that I could not figure out how they could make money. We took advantage of their offer and used them a lot at busy times and throughout Liz's illness. If we had not owned two vans then I do not think we could have handled the deliveries ourselves at such a low cost.

Once you take account of the purchase or lease costs of a van, labour, insurance, fuel, repairs and servicing, the delivery process is expensive. However, some customers think that deliveries should be free. Despite the messages promoted by some businesses, there is really no such thing as free delivery. Anyone offering this will almost always be factoring the cost of delivery into the product or service they provide. They are not deducting it from their net profit as an act of kindness. The problem with this is that customers who collect their own goods are in effect subsidising customers who receive this so-called 'free delivery'. Within government circles there are proposals to outlaw this practice so that consumers know just what they are paying for.

We charged a delivery rate that started at £3.50 for local deliveries and ranged up to £9 for the more remote villages. Interflora charged a flat rate of £4.95 per delivery. This could rise to £10 for a priority delivery that had to be delivered within three hours of the customer placing the order. Not all of this is passed on to the florist making the delivery, however. The deliverer will receive just £2.75 for a local delivery but this could rise to £7 or more for delivery to a distant village. These charges enabled us to cover all our delivery costs but we certainly did not make a profit from the delivery service.

Peak period planning

While one van may be sufficient for many shops, for handling all the deliveries on a normal day, everyone needs extra vehicles at peak times.

You can take advantage of friends and relations prepared to help out. I found this was only cost-effective if they had a suitable vehicle of their own and were suitably insured. Hiring extra vans for a day or two is relatively expensive. The best solution for us was to book our low-cost delivery service and pay them by the drop.

In the run-up to a peak period, as we took each order we would double-check the address details. These were written on the message card envelope, together with the delivery date, which was attached to the order form. At the end of each day I would go through these and write an area code in one corner of the envelope. CC for Cambridge central, CN for Cambridge North, W for a village to the west, etc. If the delivery had been guaranteed for a certain time this would be clearly marked on the envelope. If there were attachments to the order, such as balloons, chocolates, etc., this was also clearly marked on the envelope.

Once each order was made up, the florist would check that all the attachments were there. The order would be placed in a designated area corresponding to its particular area code. Every available space was used, including the office and storage sheds. Any timed deliveries would be prominently placed at the front of each batch of orders.

On peak period days I did not usually do any deliveries myself. I spent all my time organising the drivers, allocating them to the areas they were most familiar with. I helped them load the orders and make up the delivery sheets. I ensured they knew about any orders that had to be delivered by a particular time. New orders would be coming in all the time, so the situation was very fluid. Lots of make-up work would be in progress and new orders had to be placed in the correct areas. I checked and double-checked orders continually to ensure that no order had been accidentally misfiled or obscured somewhere.

As well as taking responsibility for all the orders that your shop needs to make up and deliver, you also need to keep an eye on the relay orders you have sent. These should be delivered by another florist but it is well worth doing all the checking you can. By using the Interflora computerised system we were able to check that each order we had sent really had been received and formally accepted by the executing florist.

On the day of delivery any orders that are flagged on the computer as 'Sent', rather than 'Accepted' should be checked. This means calling the executing florist and asking whether they have a problem. Often the other florist will respond by saying they are aware of the order but have not yet handled it. Unfortunately sometimes the response is along the lines of 'We are in a terrible mess with more orders than we can handle and things are out of control'.

One Valentine's Day I called a shop to query an order and my call was answered by a lady who was crying her eyes out. She said, 'It's just so busy, more and more orders keep coming in, we can't make them all, I don't think we've bought enough stock and I just can't cope.' The pressure really does tell on people.

I have always felt really sorry for any florist hit by unexpected staff absence on a peak day. I was always so grateful that our staff were so committed that they struggled in, even if they felt unwell. We all took the view that somehow we had to be at work, no matter what. A truly annoying situation is when you try to call a shop to query an order on Mother's Day and find they are closed. There are a few shops that do not even deliver on Mother's Day.

10 Handling complaints

This chapter looks at:

- Relay order complaints
- Assessing complaints
- Delivery problems
- Complaints about short product life

It is a fact of life that every florist shop receives complaints. Some are justified and some are not. No matter how good your shop and the products that leave it, there will be people who think you are absolutely useless.

You can get a bad reputation with an individual customer very easily. You may deliver a bouquet in mixed colours, because that is what the sender ordered from you, and find the recipient likes only pink flowers. This will be your fault and the recipient may vow never to use your shop again.

This particular example is taken from real experience. Some years ago the recipient received several orders from us. She complained about every single one for reasons that were often quite hilarious. On one occasion I visited her to show her an order form, as proof that we had delivered exactly what the sender had specified. I also explained to her that of the hundreds of orders we had fulfilled one Mother's Day hers was the only complaint we had received. I even asked her in all honesty if she had a grudge against us. In exasperation, we blacklisted this lady for a while and refused to accept any orders for delivery to her. Then bizarrely she did a complete volte-face and decided that everything we did was absolutely lovely!

I believe that the floristry trade is extraordinarily understanding and generous in the way it handles complaints. The compensatory action taken is often way above what anyone would reasonably expect from other industries. I sometimes wonder if we roll over too easily.

We had an occasion when we received an Interflora order for an arrangement to be delivered to someone. Having made the arrangement and tried to deliver it we found that the recipient had moved to a different part of the country some months previously. Interflora then asked us to cancel the order and re-send it to another florist. We received no payment, despite the fact that one of our staff had spent twenty minutes making the arrangement. We had wasted fuel and time trying to make the delivery and we were unable to reuse most of the flowers because the stems had been cut short and at that time we had no other orders for similar arrangements. We lost money through absolutely no fault of our own.

Situations like this make florists seethe. In fairness to Interflora, in other similar situations they at least agreed to give us some compensation for the time and the stock we had wasted.

Relay order complaints

The different relay services each have their own views on how best to handle complaints and take appropriate action. The above example is typical of what happens when a recipient has moved house, is on holiday, or has perhaps been discharged from hospital. Although it may seem very unfair, situations like this have to be considered as part of the perils of trading. But I cannot think of any other industry that would give a customer a full refund in a similar situation for something that has been custom made to the customer's specification and transported to the address they have given.

Some say that as florists we have to take the wider view. Situations like this are bound to happen from time to time, but if we penalise the customer people will be put off sending flowers at all. Their view is that it is better to accept the occasional written-off order and treat it as part of the overheads of the shop.

My view is that the least we should do is explain the situation to the customer and try to agree to a partial refund. For local orders the customer is unlikely to baulk at this. People will often apologise, say that it was no fault of ours and that a 50 per cent refund is more than fair.

I once called a customer after we had tried to deliver flowers to a friend of his who had been discharged from hospital earlier in the day. Before I could even talk about what we should do he solved the problem for me, saying that he realised it was not our fault and that the order should be cancelled and he did not expect a refund.

So it can be very frustrating when you feel that the person handling a problem within a relay organisation has simply caved in and given a customer a full refund when it is not warranted. It is easy to take the view that this person is an employee who is being paid for their work regardless of any problems. As a shop owner you take the financial hit, despite doing nothing wrong. Having said this I believe that within Interflora this situation has improved greatly. Their complaint handlers are prepared to listen to both sides of a story and then attempt to reach a compromise that is fair to all parties. Sometimes, however, you end up paying the price for somebody's unreasonable behaviour.

> I had to investigate a complaint of non-delivery made by a customer. She had ordered a vase of flowers and a balloon for her son to be delivered to the porter's lodge at a Cambridge college, and she complained that we had not done this.
>
> I knew we had delivered them and I returned to the college to find out what had happened. As I walked in I saw the flowers on the reception desk in the porter's lodge, exactly where we had left them. The porters double-checked that they had indeed left a message for the recipient to collect them.
>
> I phoned Interflora from the college to explain this and they promised to let the customer know. I subsequently found that Interflora had decided to give the customer a full refund anyway, saying that she was so angry they just could not reason with her. Interflora compensated me for our loss but I was still furious that they had backed down. Neither Interflora nor our shop had done anything wrong. The customer had her order correctly made and delivered and then used bullying tactics to get a full refund. To me this simply encourages a customer to try similar tactics again in the future.

It is all very well for Interflora to compensate shops in this sort of instance, but refunds given to customers are effectively paid for by all the Interflora member shops.

Interflora have urged all their members to agree to a 'no quibble guarantee'. There is talk of this being implemented right across the membership in the future. The positive aspect of this is that it shows quite exceptional customer service and confidence in the quality of the products supplied by member shops. The downside is that it will encourage more and more people to make unjustified complaints. The message will spread that if you place an order with Interflora, all you have to do is lodge a complaint and you will get your money back.

Teleflorist insists that its members must guarantee full customer satisfaction in delivery, quality and value or their money back. They also specify that deliveries for birthdays and anniversaries should be made in the morning or at the latest by 4pm.

These sorts of constraints could hit the small retailer hard. Giving the occasional refund on a £20 gift-wrap is not much of a problem but on Valentine's Day young lads spend literally hundreds of pounds on huge bouquets of red roses. I am pretty sure that if some of them knew about a no quibble guarantee they would be looking for a refund, no matter how good the product delivered.

My personal view is that no quibble guarantees will lead to some very unfair situations for member shops. It is one thing for Tesco to offer a seven-day guarantee for an inexpensive bunch of cut flowers. For an ordinary shop, often supplying high value products, there has to be a more reasonable process of assessing a complaint.

Assessing complaints

Every shop receives complaints – some are valid and some are not. Some flowers will not last as long as they should. Florists are only human and they make mistakes just like anyone else.

Almost any florist will quickly replace flowers or give a refund where the complaint is valid. If a regular customer said their flowers only lasted a few days there was no need for us even to see the flowers. We would apologise, supply replacements and add a complimentary box of chocolates. If the recipient was unknown to us and made a complaint relating to quality we would first request that they bring the flowers into the shop. This was so that we could check what was wrong and, if appropriate, issue a refund or supply replacements. If they said they could not get to the shop we would visit them with replacements. We would then ask to see what the problem was before handing over the replacement flowers.

There are very good reasons for asking to see what the problem is. Once a customer complained that, against her wishes, we had included roses in her order. When we saw the 'roses' they were in fact *Lisianthus*. Another customer complained that we had not included red carnations, but when we saw the bouquet the red carnations were there. It was obvious the customer did not know what carnations looked like.

> Other complaints can be less straightforward. One woman I visited lived in a large house in an expensive area of Cambridge. She complained about a £20 gift-wrap bouquet a friend had sent her. I could see nothing wrong with it and asked her explain the problem. She then admitted that the real problem was that she had been out when we made the delivery and the flowers had been left with her next-door neighbour. As someone more used to receiving a £50 hand-tied selection, she was embarrassed that the neighbours had seen that someone had sent her an obviously inexpensive bouquet. It meant loss of face with the neighbours!

Some shops take the view that the most cost-effective approach is to spend as little time as possible assessing the validity of a complaint. It is better to apologise and either replace or refund the order. There is some sense in this but personally I have always had a real problem with lying down and letting someone walk all over you.

I would usually visit the recipient personally to assess the situation. If the complaint had any validity at all we would give the recipient some form of replacement and a genuine apology that was in excess of what they had been expecting. If the complaint was a try-on we gave them nothing at all. Following one complaint of non-delivery of an order some five weeks previously, I visited the address with replacement flowers. When I got there I recognised the house and the recipients. I then remembered very clearly that when I made the delivery they were sitting in their front garden having a drink with some friends. I explained this and was even able to describe their friends. They were extremely embarrassed and apologised profusely. I took the replacement flowers back to the shop.

If a complaint relates to poor value then it is important to check what went into the order. Most florists will list the flower content and value on the order form and this is vital information in the event of a problem. Usually the content and value will prove to be correct. The problem is either the customer's perception of what a £25 bouquet should look like or that flower prices were unusually high at the time. Most people will understand why you have to charge higher prices at Valentine's Day or Mother's Day. However prices can soar at the Dutch auctions for events such as Mother's Day in Russia. This affects shops all over Europe but is much more difficult to explain to customers.

It is not a good idea to tell the customer the total flower value that should have gone into their order. They will not want to know that you

also had to pay the florist to make it, cover all the other costs of your business and make a profit. The only people who can demand to know the actual flower value is Trading Standards if a complaint has been referred to them. As they fully understand all the other costs involved, this is never a problem.

We only ever had two complaints referred to Trading Standards. On both occasions I found them completely understanding and supportive of our position. One of these complaints was from a lady who bought a large glass vase from us and then used it for three months before it developed a crack. I checked with the supplier who was adamant that this could only happen if it had been damaged in some way. Perhaps it had been in a dishwasher or someone had knocked it over? The lady was adamant that she wanted a full refund and so eventually I contacted Trading Standards for advice. They responded by saying they could not believe anyone would make such a complaint and they certainly would not expect me to make any refund.

Sometimes a recipient might ask the price of an item delivered, perhaps because they want to assess the value for money. This information should not be divulged as it could upset the sender. It is obviously not ethical to divulge what someone has spent on a gift. If the recipient is really insistent, tell them to ask the sender.

A £20 gift-wrap bouquet is far more likely to generate a complaint than a £50 hand-tied selection. Many recipients feel sure that their friend or relative will have spent a lot of money on them and when they receive a basic bouquet they are very likely to be disappointed. This is yet another reason for developing high value sales. As well as boosting your sales and profits they reduce the level of complaints.

Delivery problems

Most florists will find a neighbour willing to accept a delivery if the recipient is not at home but this can occasionally lead to problems. Many neighbours will be only too pleased to help and will often offer to put the flowers in water and keep them somewhere cool. However, some will refuse and tell you they do not get on with their neighbour and do want to do anything to help them.

I tried to deliver flowers to one address and had to visit the next-door neighbour. The door was opened by a very friendly lady with a big smile. She said she would be delighted to help. When I returned to the shop the recipient phoned to say that she had seen the card I had put through her door but would not collect her flowers. She said the neighbour was an awful woman, she did not want anything to do with her and for all she cared the flowers could rot. Luckily the neighbour decided to take the flowers round herself when she realised they were not going to be collected.

Another very angry lady complained that I had left her flowers at the house opposite but she did not know the people. She refused to cross the road to collect the flowers and wanted me to return to the house immediately – a round trip of twelve miles – and get the flowers for her. It was the end of a long day and I refused: frankly I did not care if we lost this particular customer.

Another complaint was from someone whose Valentine's Day flowers were delivered by a plain white van. They had expected one of our vans displaying the shop name and the graphics showing a bunch of flowers on the side. The customer seemed to be amazed that we had not invested in an extra six vans for the day and had them all sign-written!

Despite the occasional delivery problems I would almost always advocate finding a neighbour to leave an order with, rather than returning the order to the shop. There will be the occasional exception. Perhaps a neighbour thinks the recipient is away on holiday. My experience is that returning orders to the shop for re-delivery some time later is very expensive and time wasting.

Complaints about short product life

One of the most common complaints for any florist is that the flowers supplied did not last very long. This may or may not be valid and, as I wrote earlier, it is generally a good idea to see the flowers yourself. Try to determine exactly what has happened to them. The problem may be due to poor quality or to something the recipient has or has not done.

It is impossible to state that a certain type of flower will last a certain length of time because flower life depends on so many variables. When you purchase flowers from a wholesaler you do not know when they were cut. You do not know what sort of conditions they have been kept in since cutting. If they were fresh stock bought at auction and then promptly loaded into a refrigerated lorry that delivered them equally promptly to your shop, flower life should be good. But some wholesalers will decide that old unsold stock still looks pretty good a week later. They are then tempted to try to offload it onto an unsuspecting customer.

Most customers have no idea that their vases may contain bacteria or salt deposits from their dishwasher. When any of our customers complained that their flowers had quickly died we would replace them and take the opportunity to tell the customer that it would be a good idea to bleach their vases.

Some complaints are of course completely groundless. I remember delivering a gift-wrap bouquet to a young couple and making a further delivery to them two days later. When I made the second delivery I saw that the bouquet delivered previously was propped up against a hot radiator in the hallway, still out of water! Any flowers neglected in this way will obviously have a very short life and there is nothing the florist can do.

Conclusion

I hope that, having read this book, you will have a much better chance of making the right decisions about how to find or start a business that will provide you with a fulfilling and rewarding way of life.

Retail floristry is unlikely to make anyone particularly wealthy but it can provide a very pleasant way of life for those with the right skills and enthusiasm. I do not know of anyone who has succeeded without investing a lot of very hard work and commitment. It is a trade in which you really do have to make your own luck.

Floristry has helped me to take early retirement at the age of 56 but I already know that I miss it. I miss the fun and the banter of working with a lovely bunch of girls and I even miss the cold early mornings.

On the next Valentine's Day I will take great pleasure from having a long lie-in while I think about what it will be like in florist shops around the country. However, I suspect that in a way I will still miss the sheer dynamism and chaos of the day. I know I will miss the pleasure of adding up the takings at the end of it!

Whatever impact this book might have on the decisions you take about a future in retail floristry, I wish you all the luck in the world.

Alan Peck
Cambridge 2005

Useful contacts

Floristry courses

BCA (Berkshire College of Agriculture), Maidenhead 01628 824444
Chichester College, Pulborough 01243 786321
City College Manchester 0800 013 0123
Guildford College 01483 884000
Hadlow College, Tonbridge 0500 551434
Keits, Radlett, Herts 01923854586
Myerscough College, Preston 01995 642222
Oaklands College, St Albans 01727 737 080
Reaseheath College, Nantwich 01270 613211
Rodbaston College, Stafford 01785 712209
Writtle College, Chelmsford 01245 424200

Marketing

Flower Council of Holland, Salisbury 01722 337505/6
The Flowers and Plants Association, London 020 7738 8044

Relay services

British Teleflower Service Ltd, Romsey 01794 526460
Flowergram Ltd, Stourbridge 01384 446300
Interflora, Sleaford 01529 304141

Index